SpringerBriefs in Population Studies

For further volumes:
http://www.springer.com/series/10047

Immigrants on the steps of the Winnipeg Immigration Hall c.1900, *Library and Archives Canada*, A122676

Robert Vineberg

Responding to Immigrants' Settlement Needs: The Canadian Experience

 Springer

Robert Vineberg
Canada West Foundation
Calgary, AL
Canada

Prairie Metropolis Centre
Edmonton, AL
Canada

Canada West Foundation
900, One Lombard Place
Winnipeg MB R3B 0X3
Canada
e-mail: vineberg@cwf.ca

ISSN 2211-3215   e-ISSN 2211-3223
ISBN 978-94-007-2687-1   e-ISBN 978-94-007-2688-8
DOI 10.1007/978-94-007-2688-8
Springer Dordrecht Heidelberg London New York

Library of Congress Control Number: 2011940777

Printed on acid-free paper

Springer is part of Springer Science+Business Media (www.springer.com)

Dedication

This history of the immigration settlement services in Canada is dedicated to all those who have worked and who are working to welcome immigrants and refugees to Canada including:

Within Citizenship and Immigration Canada (CIC), the management and staff of the Integration Branch at CIC Headquarters in Ottawa, the management, program advisors and support staff at regional offices and the management, officers and support staff in CIC settlement units across the country.

Within provincial governments, settlement management, officers and support staff.

Within settlement serving agencies, the management and staff and countless volunteers who care enough to make a difference.

Within churches and other volunteer organizations, those who have sponsored refugees. To all who have made Canada a welcoming place for immigrants and refugees in the past and to all who continue to do so today, this story is for you.

Preface

I can scarcely imagine any obligation which it is more incumbent on Government to fulfill, than that of ... securing to ... persons disposed to emigrate every possible facility and assistance, from the moment of their intending to leave ... to that of their comfortable establishment...

... when the State leads great numbers of people into a situation in which it is impossible that they should do well without assistance, then the obligation to assist them begins; and it never ends, in my humble opinion, until those who have relied on the truth and paternal care of the Government, are placed in a situation to take care of themselves.[1]

John George Lambton, Earl of Durham, 1839

The concept of immigrant settlement in Canada is not new, as can be attested by the excerpt, above, from Lord Durham's famous *Report on the Affairs of British North America*. Nor have efforts to assist immigrants to Canada been only of recent date. However, interest in the welfare of immigrants has waxed and waned over the decades and centuries and it was only in 1974 that the Government of Canada finally saw fit to group its various activities in support of immigrants into an identifiable "programme for providing services to immigrants."[2]

The purpose of this history is to tell the story of immigrant settlement activities in Canada, from colonial times to the present day and to draw lessons from the past that are relevant to today. This story has its origins in the French régime and the history of the British North American colonial provinces. The concept of immigrant settlement is not new but it has evolved enormously over time.

This history is of the government response to the settlement needs of immigrants to the northern part of North America that is now Canada. It is not intended to be a history of Canadian settlement movements, nor of Canadian settlement serving organizations. Those stories, well worth telling, are for other times and other places.

Acknowledgments

I would like to thank all those who have contributed to the creation of this history of the Settlement Program:

Les Linklater, Assistant Deputy Minister, Strategic and Program Policy and Deborah Tunis, Director General, Integration Branch, Citizenship and Immigration Canada (CIC), who supported an earlier version of this history and arranged, for me, access to certain archives and CIC files.

Dr. Caroline Andrew, Director of the Centre on Governance at the School of Political Studies at the University of Ottawa, who provided financial support for an earlier version of this history.

John Biles, Special Advisor to the Director General, Integration Branch, for his encouragement and insight.

Dr. Brian Gushulak, formerly of the Immigration Health Programs Branch, CIC, for sharing his knowledge of the history of public and immigrant health programs.

Staff of the Library and Archives of Canada, who have been uniformly helpful in assisting me in accessing original documents in the possession of the archives.

Staff of the Archives of Manitoba who have been equally helpful.

Dr. Lori Wilkinson, Associate Professor of Sociology, University of Manitoba, who arranged for me to have access to the resources of the University of Manitoba Library.

Dr. Baha Abu-Laban, Professor Emeritus of Sociology and Director Emeritus, Prairie Metropolis Centre, University of Alberta, who encouraged me to seek publication of this work.

Dr. Lena Horne, my partner, and Associate Professor of Textile Sciences, University of Manitoba, whose encouragement has inspired me and whose academic rigour has set a very high standard to emulate.

My thanks go to all those I have mentioned but the responsibility for this history, the opinions expressed and any errors it may contain, rests solely with me.

Robert Vineberg

Introduction

There is a great deal of literature about Canada's modern settlement program and a growing body of research and analysis of the settlement and integration successes and challenges of recent years. However, there is virtually no literature that has addressed the history of settlement services since the beginning of immigration to this country. Some survey histories of Canadian immigration have touched on elements of settlement policy but no history of services to immigrants in Canada has been published heretofore. This book is intended to begin to fill this gap in the historiography of Canadian immigration. From the tentative steps taken by the pre-Confederation colonies to provide for the needs of arriving immigrants, often sick and destitute, through the provision of accommodation and free land to settlers of a century ago, to today's multi-faceted settlement program, this book traces a fascinating history that provides an important context to today's policies and practices. It also serves to remind us that those who preceded us did, indeed, care for immigrants; did indeed understand the contribution immigrants could make to the building of this nation; and, did much to make them feel welcome in Canada.

As Lord Durham wrote, so eloquently, almost two centuries ago, it is incumbent upon any state that seeks to attract immigrants to provide them with "every possible facility and assistance" and this obligation does not cease until the immigrants are settled successfully. At many times, in its history, Canada failed to provide its immigrants with that necessary assistance and not only did immigrants suffer but so did Canadians. If there is any lesson to be drawn from the history of Canada's immigration experience, it is that settlement services provide, not only for the well-being of immigrants but also contribute to the well-being of the host country. Immigrants who integrate well into the economic, social and cultural tapestry of their new home contribute to the financial, intellectual and spiritual wealth of their new nation. Countries, whose immigrants who do not integrate well, will face enormous social, economic and political problems.

Canada's history of immigrant settlement is unique to itself but there are universal lessons to be learned from the long experience Canada has had with immigrant settlement. First and foremost, immigrant settlement is a symbiotic relationship that benefits both the newcomer and the host country and its residents.

If a country decides to seek migrants, it will need to plan a settlement program to be ready to provide needed services, ideally, even before the arrival of the first immigrants. The Canadian story is marked by many tremendous successes: free accommodation and free land, in the early years, and language and occupational training combined with orientation and counselling programs in recent years, to mention just a few. However, at times, we have faltered. We have allowed successful programs to atrophy; we have discontinued programs without reference to any objective criteria; and we grossly underfunded our settlement programs in the 1990s and early 2000s, even as we admitted immigrants at near historically high levels.

Canada is, of course, a federal state and our *Constitution Act* actually defines immigration as a shared jurisdiction between the federal and provincial governments. More and more, in Canada and elsewhere, we are rediscovering the fact that immigrants integrate into communities first and nations only later. The role that municipalities are assuming in immigrant settlement is welcome and necessary and co-ordination among all levels of government is a necessary requirement for successful immigrant settlement. But it is not sufficient. Settlement service providers, other non-governmental organizations and the general public all have an important role to play.

The lessons to be learned from Canada's immigrant settlement experience have implications not only in Canada but in other immigrant receiving jurisdictions as well. It is my hope that this book will be of interest to anyone interested in this field, whether they be policy makers, program analysts, practitioners, researchers, students or an informed member of the general public. And I hope that this history will be of interest, not only for those who work in immigration settlement today and in the future but for all who may be interested in how Canada has welcomed its future citizens throughout its history.

Contents

Chapter 1
Pre-Confederation Settlement Activities

In the Beginning

It can be argued that the first immigrant settlement services were offered by
Canada's aboriginal First Nations peoples on the arrival of the early French and
English settlers. Without their assistance and without recourse to their skills in living
in a sometimes hostile northern climate, it is unlikely the first European arrivals
would have survived. However, the French, in particular, learned quickly from their
"hosts" and also, very practically, intermarried, creating the Métis people.

During the French regime, total immigration from Europe was very small—
perhaps 30,000 in 150 years—and it mostly consisted of demobilized French
soldiers who were offered land in New France and Acadia as well as women who
came to join them or indentured servants destined to households in New France.[1]
Therefore settlement services, as such, were not needed.

Following the Seven Years War and the French cession of Canada and Acadia
to Britain in 1763, the British, at first, repeated the French pattern of settlement by
providing free land to demobilized soldiers of the many regiments who fought in
the War. Free land, was, again, the major settlement tool when, following the
American War of Independence, large numbers of "United Empire Loyalists"
moved north to the surviving British North American colonies.

Protect the Emigrant; Protect Yourself

The earliest proactive settlement activities in the British North American colonies
were aimed, as much at protecting the existing citizens of the provinces as helping
the new immigrants to establish themselves. The three provinces with major ports
(Lower Canada, New Brunswick and Nova Scotia) all adopted *Quarantine Acts*
that provided that all ships carrying diseased passengers had to wait off shore for

R. Vineberg, *Responding to Immigrants' Settlement Needs: The Canadian Experience*,
SpringerBriefs in Population Studies, DOI: 10.1007/978-94-007-2688-8_1,
© The Author(s) 2012

medical clearance. In 1761, Nova Scotia passed its first act regarding *Distempers, to prevent the spreading thereof* and in 1795, Lower Canada passed a *Quarantine Act*, requiring "ships and vessels coming from places infected with the plague or any pestilential fever or disease, to perform *Quarantine,* and prevent the communication thereof".[2] While these acts affected immigrants, they were not directed specifically at immigrants.

The bulk of immigrants, in the early 1800s, were Scots, and a Committee of the British House of Commons was struck to look into issues affecting Scotland, including emigration. It observed, "That Persons emigrating from different Parts of the United Kingdom, have in various Instances, suffered great Distress and Hardship, on account of the crowded State of the Vessels, the want of a sufficient stock of Provisions, Water, and other Necessaries for the Voyage, and in various other Respects". Therefore, the committee recommended, "That, it is expedient to regulate Vessels carrying Passengers from the United Kingdom to His Majesty's Plantations and Settlements abroad, or to Foreign Parts, with respect to the Number of Passengers which they shall be allowed to take on board, in proportion to the Tonnage of such Vessels, as well as with respect to the Provision of proper Necessaries for the Voyage".[3]

In response to the report, the first *Passenger Act* was passed, by the Imperial Parliament, in 1803.[4] Healthy immigrants were more likely to survive and succeed but, more importantly, healthy immigrants were not going to infect the British North American population with disease. However, as the *Passenger Act* restricted the number of emigrants per tonnage of the vessel, it forced prices up and, temporarily, discouraged emigration. Also, throughout the Napoleonic Wars and for a few years following, the British Government did not encourage emigration for fear of losing military manpower.

The *Passenger Act* was repealed in 1827, but as many ship owners soon reverted to their old ways, a new *Passenger Act* was passed the following year.[5] However, abuses continued and the British North American provinces complained to the Colonial Office. In response, on December 11, 1831, the Colonial Secretary, Lord Goderich, wrote to the Lt. Governors of Lower Canada, Nova Scotia and New Brunswick to suggest that it would be appropriate for the provinces to impose a small tax upon all emigrants both to help keep ships' masters in line but also "to raise a fund applicable to the expense of receiving and forwarding emigrants to the places of their destination" and "in supporting hospitals in the ports where emigrants arrive (thus relieving the inhabitants from the burthen to which they are now exposed), and in defraying other necessary expenses".[6] All three provinces gladly accepted the advice of Lord Goderich. The Nova Scotia *Act relating to Passengers from Great-Britain and Ireland, arriving in this Province* was typical of all three. Section V of the *Act* specifically provided authority to "draw from the Treasury, from time to time, all or any such Monies and to pay and apply the same in such manner, and to such uses and purposes, for the benefit of poor Emigrants arriving in this Province..." Section II of the *Act* provided for the financing of these activities by imposing a fee per immigrant that ships' masters or owners had to pay on arrival in Nova Scotia before immigrants could be landed. If the ship's

Fig. 1.1 Grosse Ile Quarantine station 2nd class hotel c1905 *Library and Archives Canada* C079029

master had obtained, before embarkation, a certificate from the port authorities in Great Britain or Ireland that every passenger had been "embarked by and with the sanction of His Majesty's Government", the fee would be five shillings per adult passenger. However, if even one passenger had not been properly embarked, the fee was ten shillings for every passenger. Furthermore, Section VII provided that if passengers were landed before entry had been granted, the ship's master would be fined ten pounds for every passenger landed illegally. The Nova Scotia legislation was approved on February 16, 1832. Within eleven days, both Lower Canada (on February 25) and New Brunswick (on February 27) had approved similar legislation.[7] Upper Canada, without the benefit of a seaport where a head tax could be imposed, had to allocate £250 in 1832 for the relief of emigrants arriving at Prescott as they made their way up the St. Lawrence River.[8]

However, notwithstanding the *Passenger Acts*, many immigrants arrived in poor health largely due to the continuing overcrowding on vessels which made the voyage more profitable for the ship owners. Similarly, respecting quarantine meant delay and, for ships' masters, delay was money lost, so the requirement was honoured in the breach despite the threat of heavy fines.

In 1831, when a major cholera epidemic struck in England and was carried to British North America by emigrant ships, the following year, the death toll at the quarantine stations was immense and, still, the epidemic reached Canadian shores. The 1832 legislation in the three provinces had been passed in anticipation of the epidemic and funds raised from the landing fee (or head tax) were immediately needed. Already, volunteer-organized emigrant aid societies had been established in many places, with the largest being in Québec City and Montréal. However, much of the work of those two societies was designed to hurry immigrants off to Upper Canada or the United States so they would not settle and become public charges in either of those cities. But the emigrant aid societies were always short of funds and the head taxes helped defray their expenses.

In the face of the epidemic, quarantine legislation in all three provinces was strengthened in 1832 and 1833[9] and temporary quarantine facilities for Lower Canada, established at Grosse Ile, downstream of Québec were made permanent (Fig. 1.1). In New Brunswick, Partridge Island, at the mouth of Saint John harbour had been identified as a quarantine site for New Brunswick in 1809 but was first used in 1830. Nova Scotia relied on quarantine aboard ships until the cholera epidemic of 1866 when the provincial government purchased Lawlor's Island in Halifax harbour. This station was finally opened by the government of the new Dominion of Canada in 1868.[10]

Other developments were taking place at the same period. In 1823, Lower Canada appropriated funds to establish an immigrant hospital in Québec City,[11] and in 1827 the Colonial Office appointed a Chief Emigration Agent at Québec City. His duties were "to receive emigrants on landing, give out landing money, if any, clothe and feed the starving, hear complaints and bring proceedings against defaulting shipmasters, keep in touch with those needing employment, help newcomers to find their friends and transship them to their destination, and have all carefully recorded".[12] This was all very good in theory, but beyond a very basic service, the Chief Emigration Agent was quite limited in what he could achieve.

Lord Durham's famous *Report on the Affairs of British North America* is better known for its commentary on Canadian politics and the recommendations that led to the union of Upper and Lower Canada. However, he addressed the issue of emigration in quite some detail. He dealt at some length regarding the violations of the *Passenger Act* and the consequences for the emigrants and Canadians. With respect to the Chief Emigration Agent's enormous mandate, Lord Durham commented:

> However defective the present arrangements for the passage of emigrants, they are not more so than the means employed to provide for the comfort and prosperity of this class after their arrival in the Colonies. Indeed, it may be said that no such means are in existence. It will be seen, from the very meager evidence of the Agent for Emigrants at Québec, that the office which he holds is next to useless. I cast no blame on the officer, but would only explain, that he has no powers, nor scarcely any duties to perform. Nearly all that is done for the advantage of poor emigrants, after they have passed the Lazaretto [quarantine station], is performed by the Québec and Montreal Emigrants Societies— benevolent associations of which I am bound to speak in the highest terms of commendation; to which, indeed, we owe whatever improvement has taken place in the yet unhealthy mid-passage, but which, as they were instituted for the main purpose of relieving the inhabitants of the two cities from the miserable spectacle of crowds of unemployed and starving emigrants, so have their efforts produced little other good than that of facilitating the progress of poor emigrants to the United States ...[13]

Durham concluded his views on emigration by observing that, "I object ...only to such emigration as now takes place—without forethought, preparation, method or system of any kind".[14] Lord Durham's views as to what ought to be done are cited in the preface to this history.

Unfortunately, not much changed in subsequent years. The numbers of poor immigrants increased as the British *Poor Law Relief Act* was amended in 1834 to allow parishes to raise funds to send the poor to the colonies.[15] This money included "landing money" to help the new arrivals to establish themselves. In Canada, the Chief Emigration Agent distributed this landing money, at Québec City and at sub-offices established in Montreal, Kingston, Toronto and Hamilton and other cities. And the Potato Famines in Ireland increased this movement enormously in the 1840s.

The Parliament of the new Province of Canada, in its first parliamentary session, in 1841, passed legislation to assist indigent immigrants, modeled on the earlier Lower Canada legislation but, again, not much changed in approach.[16] On attainment of responsible government in 1848, the first legislation passed by the Province of Canada was another bill to assist indigent immigrants. The main differences from earlier legislation were that it doubled the head tax from five to ten shillings and it authorized the Medical Superintendent of Quarantine to examine all immigrants on arrival.[17] The following year, a similar act was passed, modifying the fee structure to seven shillings and six pence per adult and five shillings for those between the ages of five and fifteen.[18] This was an important provision as ships' masters often falsified the ages of young adults to avoid the fees. The fees were subsequently lowered to five shillings for adults and three shillings and nine pence, for children, in order to remain competitive in the immigrant business.

In 1852, the Province of Canada passed legislation to consolidate the laws respecting emigrants and quarantine, thus emphasizing the important link between the two functions.[19] This act was amended in 1858 by a short, four page act that introduced several significant changes. In particular, the landing fee was made a consistent five shillings per head for everyone over the age of one. Experience had proven that ships' masters were reporting almost every young adult as under fifteen to take advantage of the lower fee for children. The act also required anyone, within a five mile radius of the ports of Québec and Montréal, seeking to advise emigrants for gain, lodge them or sell them passage onward had to be licensed by the mayor, on recommendation of the Chief Agent for Emigration in that municipality. Finally, the act required every innkeeper in any city, town or village designated by the Governor in Council to "cause to be kept conspicuously posted in the public rooms and passages of his house and printed upon business cards, a list of the rates of prices which will be charged Emigrants per day and week for board or lodging, or both, and also the rates for separate meals…" and the cards had to be given to immigrants immediately on arrival.[20] For the first time, Canadian immigration legislation was specifically concerned for the welfare of immigrants in their own right as opposed to only when their ill-health might harm Canadian residents.

The *Act Respecting emigrants and quarantine* was amended and consolidated one final time by the Province of Canada in 1866. The landing fee was now stipulated in the more common currency in British North America—the dollar— and it was set at $1 per person for those with proper departure papers and $1.50 for those without proper departure sanction.[21]

Chapter 2
Post-Confederation Settlement Activities to 1945

Sorting Out the Jurisdictions

Section 95 of the *Constitution Act*, originally known as the *British North America Act* (*BNA Act*), conferred concurrent jurisdiction on the provincial and Dominion governments for immigration and agriculture. Therefore, all the provinces were entitled, under the *BNA Act*, to engage in immigration. The 1868 *Canada Year Book*, printed summaries of immigration practices in the three founding provinces:

> Canada [Ontario and Québec] has for a long period endeavoured to afford to the emigrating classes in Great Britain and several other European countries, correct information respecting the position and resources of the country, the wages obtainable and the cost of living; to give to emigrants on their arrival, the advantage of official and therefore disinterested advice as to the places where employment is to be found, which information is obtained from officials stationed in the principal cities; also to furnish information as to the quantity, quality, and price of Crown lands open for settlement in the various districts. The tax payable by masters of vessels for emigrants on arriving has of late years been reduced, and it is now $1 per head for emigrants in ships, under the sanction of British officials, and $1.50 for others. During 1866 and 1867, it has published and circulated extensively in England, a valuable newspaper called "The Canada Emigration Gazette," filled with the information likely to be required by persons desirous of changing their abode from England to Canada.
>
> Nova Scotia has made no organized efforts in this direction until lately. It now grants passages to Halifax through its shipping agents in England on payment of twenty shillings. No head money or tax is levied on emigrants arriving, and a credit of 3 years is given them on the purchase of Crown lands in a tract set apart for them.
>
> In New Brunswick, the Government has occasionally sent a travelling or lecturing agent to Britain, and has published several admirable essays on the resources of the Province.[1]

Clearly, adequate information on immigration was becoming a major settlement tool. While much information was available, promoters and shipping agents tended to paint a far rosier picture than was the reality of immigrating to a frontier country and the government wanted accurate information to be available.

R. Vineberg, *Responding to Immigrants' Settlement Needs: The Canadian Experience*, SpringerBriefs in Population Studies, DOI: 10.1007/978-94-007-2688-8_2,
© The Author(s) 2012

Fig. 2.1 Immigrant shed at
Lévis, Québec, c.1860,
*Library and Archives
Canada*, A165571

Given the concurrent jurisdiction, it was important to sort out the jurisdictional issues involving immigration and a Dominion-provincial conference took place on October 30, 1868 to that end. It was at the highest level, with Prime Minister, Sir John A. Macdonald, heading the Dominion delegation. While many decisions were taken with respect to delivery of the immigration program, the only decisions of consequence to the health and care of immigrants was that the Dominion would assume responsibility for the quarantine stations at Québec, Halifax and Saint John and that national immigration legislation would be prepared for Parliament at the earliest possible date.[2]

Accordingly, *An Act respecting immigration and immigrants*, was introduced in the House of Commons on May 26, 1869, received second reading three days later and sent to Committee of the Whole which reviewed it on June 2. The bill was given third reading later the same day and received Royal Assent on June 22.[3] Beyond reflecting the arrangements agreed to at the conference, its provisions were little changed from the pre-Confederation Province of Canada legislation.[4] However, the attitudinal change was enormous and is seen in the new title of the legislation. It was about *immigrants*; not *emigrants*. It was about people Canada wanted; not people another country sent to Canada.

Dominion Government Initiatives

While the various colonial provinces had basically seen it necessary to care for emigrants in order to protect the general population, the new Dominion government saw that the way to build a nation and, in particular, to populate the vast western territories that it obtained in 1870 was to ensure that the immigrant got to his eventual place of settlement cheaply, comfortably and safely. To that end, the government began a program of building up the infrastructure of the immigration service in general and its capacity to assist in the settlement of immigrants in particular Figs. 2.1, 2.2.

One of the false starts was the Immigrant Aid Societies Act of 1872.[5] This act authorized over 70 districts across Canada where the establishment of immigrant aid societies would be supported and the societies would begin to take on the role

Fig. 2.2 Immigrant shed at the Forks, Winnipeg, *Archives of Manitoba*, Bole, Elswood 6, N13803

of attracting immigrants to different parts of Canada and finding work or farm-steads for them. The legislation also empowered the societies to extend loans for passage and to sue for recovery of the funds if they were not repaid. It seems that the legislation, which had been championed by the Ottawa Valley Immigration Aid Society, was only used once, in 1901, and languished on the statute book until repealed over a century after it was enacted. Most immigrant aid societies operated outside the authority of the Act without any problem.[6]

One of the best initiatives was establishing a network of "Immigration Halls" across Canada. These halls not only served as offices for immigration agents but also provided temporary housing for immigrants. In 1872, there were immigration stations with immigration halls in Québec, Montréal, Ottawa, Kingston, Toronto and Hamilton and halls were under construction in London and Winnipeg.[7] The Winnipeg "immigration sheds," as they were originally called, were built at the Forks of the Red and Assiniboine Rivers because, before the railway reached Winnipeg, immigrants arrived by riverboat from the United States. The sheds were constructed to accommodate 250 immigrants but this was not enough and the following year, they were doubled in size. With the arrival of the Canadian Pacific Railway (CPR), in 1881, the first of several increasingly large immigration halls, as they came to be called, was built in the area of the CPR station and the sheds at the Forks were demolished shortly after. Winnipeg became the hub of the western settlement operations and all immigrants heading west were de-trained in Winnipeg and given the opportunity to choose a final destination and obtain land grants. Therefore, larger facilities were required. In 1890 a more permanent hall was built and in 1906 a magnificent stone and brick immigration hall was built beside the CPR's grand new station in Winnipeg. The immigration hall not only provided modern accommodation for upwards of 500 immigrants but also served as the headquarters for the immigration service in Western Canada. The older, 1890 structure was moved beside the new hall and provided lodging to "foreign"

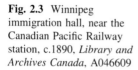

Fig. 2.3 Winnipeg immigration hall, near the Canadian Pacific Railway station, c.1890, *Library and Archives Canada*, A046609

immigrants while the newer building was reserved for "British immigrants".[8] By 1911, the *New York Times* reported, "There are throughout Western Canada some fifty Immigration Halls … each a centre of employment and land acquirement information for the new settler, and a comfortable abiding place until he is passed along to his ultimate place of settlement. Beds and bedding are provided for those who must wait overnight …"[9] Appendix 1 provides more detail on this largely forgotten Canadian initiative Figs. 2.3, 2.4.

The Dominion government also assigned immigrant agents,

> "to travel on immigrant trains, in order to see that the wants of Immigrants are duly cared for, to see that they are sent to their proper destinations, to protect them from imposition on the way, to give advice to them, to explain to them the labour wants of the country and generally to set forth the advantages of Canada as a land for settlement".[10]

From the piers at Halifax, Saint John or Québec to the railway platforms in Toronto and Winnipeg and Edmonton, fast talking swindlers were, everywhere, trying to separate newcomers from their life savings and the government worked assiduously to protect and encourage the immigrants it had attracted.

The Dominion government made arrangements with the railways and shipping agents to recruit immigrants in Europe by means of paying a bonus of about £1 per farmer or farm worker, but in the early years, following Confederation, the results were meagre. The conditions for successfully attracting large numbers to Canada were not yet in place. Indeed a large number of immigrants coming to North America via Canada were taking advantage of subsidized immigrant fares that Canada offered only to move on to the United States. Also, during the slow economic growth in the 1870s and 1880s, many Canadians looked south for a better life.

It was only in the 1890s that all the requisite conditions fell into place. First, the CPR was completed in 1886; second the Department of Agriculture developed faster maturing strains of wheat, reducing the risk of losing crops to frost; and third, the great plains of the United States were more or less full, so emigrants had to look north for free land. Finally, the European economy improved, allowing more people to afford the cost of moving to North America. In the 1893 *Annual Report* of the Department of the Interior for 1893, A.M. Burgess, the Deputy Minister, reported that he foresaw the end of the lean years for immigration:

> The rapid increase of the emigration of farmers from the United States to Manitoba and the North-west goes a long way to prove … that the limit of free land in that country which is

Fig. 2.4 A typical
immigration hall, Medicine
Hat, Alberta c.1904, *Library
and Archives Canada*,
A046342

fit for ordinary farming purposes has been reached, and that now the Canadian Northwest contains the only extensive tract of productive land on the North American continent which is open for free homesteading. Not only, therefore, may the stream of land seekers from the United States be expected to grow, but the current of that class of immigrants from other countries who are looking for farming lands will be turned more distinctly towards this country.[11]

The Last Best West

In 1896, the Liberal Government under Wilfrid Laurier took power at the most propitious of times, especially for immigration. Laurier appointed Clifford Sifton as Minister of the Interior. Sifton was born in Ontario, but moved to the booming western Manitoba city of Brandon as a young man. He was drawn to politics and became a Minister in the provincial government before moving to federal politics. As Minister of the Interior, he was determined to fill the vast prairies of Canada's west with European and American settlers. His programs and his support of extensive promotion of Canada in the United Kingdom, the United States and in continental Europe as the "Last Best West" resulted in the greatest flood of immigrants Canada has known, peaking in 1913 at over 400,000, drawn by free land and an immigration service that truly believed that it was nation building. Though Frank Oliver, another westerner, became Minister in 1905 and did not approve of the immigration from Central and Eastern Europe that Sifton had encouraged, the surge of immigration continued and grew continuously until brought to a halt in August 1914 by the onset of the First World War. However, American immigrants continued to come in large numbers until the United States joined the war in 1917.

In addition to the very personalized service the Immigration Branch was able to offer, the government also supported a growing number of non-governmental agencies in their work of attracting and helping to settle immigrants. Annual grants were provided to groups such as the Salvation Army, the Ottawa Valley

Immigration Aid Society, the Western Canadian Immigration Association, the Women's National Immigration Society and the Girl's Home of Welcome in Winnipeg. The Western Canadian Immigration Association received $1,000 in 1897 but by 1904 it received $10,000 over a two year period.[12] It seems that the multi-year contract for service providers is not a modern innovation after all!

However, not surprisingly, there was concern that the cost of supporting immigrants, who often arrived with very little, was imposing an undue burden on the Canadian taxpayer. Also, the very success Canada was having in attracting immigrants allowed it to set a higher bar. Therefore, the 1906 *Immigration Act* did not provide for a landing fee, as in the past, but introduced a provision allowing regulations to "provide as a condition to permission to enter Canada that immigrants shall possess money to a prescribed minimum amount, which amount may vary according to the class and destination of such immigrant, and otherwise according to the circumstances".[13] This was the beginning of the requirement that immigrants arrive with adequate funds to settle in Canada that continues to this day. The provision, implemented in 1908, required every adult immigrant arriving in the spring or summer to have $25 in his possession and, recognizing the greater difficulty to find work or establish on a farm in the winter, $50 if arriving in the fall or winter.[14]

All the investment in infrastructure was now paying off. The Immigration Service established Winnipeg as the "choke point" and distribution centre of immigrants to the west. The *New York Times* reported in 1911 that:

> Winnipeg is the distributing centre for Western settlers. They pour out through the great [CPR] station into the adjoining huge Immigration Hall, where they undergo inspection once more. Before they left the ship they had been inspected closely by immigration agents, and again in Montreal they had undergone careful scrutiny, so this is the third time. If they are intending homesteaders, seeking Government farms, the plans and details are all there in the Government land office, with courteous officials to help them understand. If they are workers seeking employment, there has been gathered for their information the latest reports on demand for labor in the various sections. For the small capitalist the Canadian Pacific's huge land grants cut up into sections are for sale in the building on the other side, with various attractions to make them acceptable.
>
> One of the latest, for instance, is the "ready-made" farm. The intending settler can buy, on the installment principle, a quarter or half section already fenced, with the well dug, a temporary farmhouse and barn built, part of the land already plowed and his crop put in ..."[15]

The Immigration Service took an active interest in all immigrants for their first year in Canada, often providing seed to settlers if crops failed and continuing to provide advice and encouragement through its network of immigration halls Figs. 2.5, 2.6 and 2.7.

Between the Wars

Following the First World War and the recession that immediately followed, the Canadian economy recovered and with that recovery, immigration resumed in large numbers. The government had anticipated this and, in 1917, created the

Fig. 2.5 Winnipeg Immigration Hall, No. 1, with CPR tracks in foreground, *Archives of Manitoba*, Architectural Survey-Winnipeg-Maple St/1 28/69 N21668

Fig. 2.6 Winnipeg Immigration Hall, No. 1, interior, *Library and Archives Canada*, C075993

Department of Immigration and Colonization. Though Canada had become an industrialized nation during the war, immigration policy remained focused on bringing in settlers both to open up new land and to take over farms whose owners or their children had moved to Canada's growing cities. However, though their own cities were growing, Canadians watched with a combination of fascination and horror as American cities such as New York and Chicago become infamous for over-crowding, crime and corruption. Canadians and Canadian policy makers assumed that this was due to unchecked immigration to American cities and they were determined to prevent that from happening in Canada. Therefore the focus of recruitment and settlement of immigrants was on the farm.

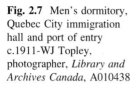 **Fig. 2.7** Men's dormitory, Quebec City immigration hall and port of entry c.1911-WJ Topley, photographer, *Library and Archives Canada*, A010438

This approach was reflected in the report of Deputy Minster W. J. Egan in the 1924–1925 *Annual Report* of the Department of Immigration and Colonization. Egan stated that "Colonization rather than immigration is the most pressing need of the hour and colonization always involves directional effort and after-care; sometimes it necessitates assistance in land purchase …" The focus was also, increasingly, on immigration "of the right type"[16] and that meant British or American, but not solely. In 1925, the Minister of Immigration and Colonization entered into a joint agreement with both the CPR and the Canadian National Railway (CNR). The "Railways Agreement" authorized the two railways to recruit and select "agriculturalists, agricultural workers and domestic servants" and settle them in Canada with the assistance of the Department of Immigration and Colonization.[17] So, *de facto*, the two railway companies ran Canada's immigrant selection system, particularly on the European Continent, and took a large part of the responsibility for settling immigrants in the Canadian west for the rest of the decade.

The British government was also actively encouraging emigration from the British Isles in the 1920s and, in 1924, the *Empire Settlement Agreement* was concluded and it provided for enormous subsidies (paid by the Canadian and British governments) for British farmers to relocate to Canada. The arrangements were complicated but the House of Commons Select Standing Committee on Agriculture and Colonization, in a 1928 report on immigration, tried to provide a simple summary of the provisions. It reported that while the normal ocean passage for immigrants from England to Canada was $91.25 (£18 15s), British agricultural workers and their wives needed to pay only $9.73 (£2). Children under 17 were free and loans were available if the immigrant could not afford even the subsidized fare. Furthermore there were special schemes whereby the British government provided $1,500 (£300) for stock and equipment and, under one scheme, provincial governments provided free land as well. By contrast, for an immigrant coming from other Northern European countries, there were no subsidies and the minimum ocean passage was $120. From Central and Southern European

countries only agricultural workers or domestic servants and those with close
relatives in Canada were eligible to immigrate to Canada and the minimum ocean
passage was $135.[18]

The major group encouraged, other than agricultural workers, was domestic
servants and they too, largely, came from the United Kingdom. The department
was assiduous in trying to ensure that these, often young, women would not be
corrupted in Canada. In 1919, it established a Women's Branch with the express
purpose to ensure "that women and children migrating to Canada might receive
the necessary advice, care, and protection." The women were interviewed in the
UK by a Women's Branch officer (all female) and they attended all embarkations
as well. At Québec, Halifax and Saint John, a Women's Branch officer met every
ship on arrival and Red Cross nursing stations were located in the immigration
buildings at the three ports as well. There were female "conductresses" on the
trains too. At major destinations, there was a "Canadian Women's Hostel" to
provide safe, accommodation pending placement with a family and assistance was
provided by the Traveller's Aid, the Young Women's Christian Association
(YWCA), the Red Cross and the Imperial Order Daughters of the Empire (IODE).
[19] There were not to be any fallen women among the immigration movement
Figs. 2.8, 2.9 and 2.10!

As a result of the emphasis on agricultural immigration in the 1920s, the focus
of immigration was still settlement in the West. To that end, while many immigration halls had closed during the war, they continued to thrive on the Prairies and
Winnipeg remained the hub. The second immigration hall in Winnipeg, closed
during the war, was renovated and reopened and then a third was built (at the
expense of the CNR) to handle the arrivals at its Winnipeg station. The secondary
hub was in Edmonton from where immigrants were being directed to the new farm
areas opening up to the north of that city. The other halls were located in communities near areas of settlement and this changed over time. The number of
people accommodated in the immigration halls, usually for an average of four to
5 days before moving onward, was impressive. The following table provides data

Fig. 2.9 "Immigration and its requirements," cartoon c 1920 by Arthur George Racey, McCord Museum, Montreal, M2005 23 236

Fig. 2.10 Immigrants arriving at the port of Quebec, c. 1925, *Library and Archives Canada*, C019935

on only the larger immigration halls. Smaller ones operated in places such as Emerson MB, North Portal SK, West Poplar River SK, Athabaska AB, Edson AB and Spirit River AB (Table 2.1)[20].

The heyday of the immigration halls was prior to the Great Depression, but many continued to function into the 1950s, providing accommodation for Hungarian refugees, for example, and those in Winnipeg and at the ports of Halifax, Québec and Vancouver continued to operate into the 1960s.

Canada no longer operates immigration halls, staffed by government employees. However, though the *Resettlement Assistance Plan*, Citizenship and Immigration Canada funds several "reception houses" in major centres across Canada, including

Table 2.1 People accommodated at immigration halls 1924–1928

Location	1924–1925	1925–1926	1926–1927	1927–1928
Winnipeg hall No. 1	4,097	5,533	9,232	8,494
Winnipeg hall No. 2	3,328	7,743	6,710	5,718
Winnipeg hall No. 3			1,952	10,973
Edmonton	1,661	2,520	6,830	4,739
Prince Albert SK	227	148	750	745
North Battleford SK	227	*Not reported*	516	591
Peace river AB	40	34	8	223
Grand Prairie AB	25	50	168	338

Winnipeg, to provide short term accommodation to Government Assisted Refugees when they first arrive in Canada. These reception houses are operated by not-for-profit immigrant settlement serving agencies. So the concept that worked so successfully in Canada's early days is kept alive in modern refugee programs.

The department also followed up regularly with new agricultural workers. This service was known as "After-Care." It was provided by the Land Settlement Branch to all migrants selected for settlement by the department. After-care consisted of:

(a) Securing employment for the migrant and directing to destination;
(b) Visiting the migrant during the first year and at least annually thereafter for a period of 5 years from the date of settlement;
(c) Hearing and dealing with any complaints regarding wages or treatment;
(d) Investigating grievances and where necessary, finding alternative employment;
(e) "Developing" a migrant, with a view to his subsequent settlement on a farm.[21]

The department had a clear vision of its settlement role and was "hands on" in carrying it out.

Support of immigrants by the voluntary sector also grew with the increase in immigration. Deputy Minister Egan, in his account, in the 1926–1927 *Annual Report*, noted that:

> The organizations continue to increase and they undoubtedly do valuable work in giving the stranger advice and a helping hand after his arrival in Canada and just when he needs help most. An extension of such voluntary effort to all settlers regardless of the country from which they came would be very helpful to the settlers and would undoubtedly provide a new impetus to future immigration.[22]

Unfortunately, the Great Depression intervened and immigration declined precipitously throughout the 1930s and then was cut off, except from the United States, during the Second World War. The settlement work continued at a much reduced scale, in proportion to the reduced immigrant flows, and staff were assigned to anti-depression reconstruction activities. As a result, in 1936, the Department of Immigration and Colonization was reduced to a branch within the new Department of Mines and Resources.

Chapter 3
The Settlement Service and the Citizenship Branch

What would become the Settlement Service grew out of previous settlement activities and functioned continuously, with the exception of the war years. Immediately, after the Second World War, former settlement staff helped relocate returning servicemen and women and then returned to their original role when immigration resumed.

In 1947, Canada's first *Citizenship Act* came into force and, given the postwar resurgence of immigration, the government decided to create a Department of Citizenship and Immigration bringing together, for the first time, immigration programs, citizenship programs and citizenship registration. The new department commenced operation in January 1950. The Citizenship Branch (as opposed to the Citizenship Registration Branch) provided financial assistance to provinces delivering language training to immigrants and assisted voluntary organizations involved in immigrant counselling and adjustment.[1]

The Settlement Service had been formally established as such in 1949 within the Immigration Branch of the Department of Mines and Resources. It moved, with the rest of the Immigration Branch, to the new Department of Citizenship and Immigration in 1950. As well as counseling and assistance in Canada, the role of the Settlement Service also involved promotion and recruitment abroad. The 1953 *Canada Year Book* offered a succinct description of the role of the Settlement Service:

> Of increasing importance is the work of the Settlement Service, which has staffs [sic] in all provinces of Canada and in the British Isles. The Settlement Officers in Canada locate and develop opportunities for immigrants in accordance with the needs of the areas under their supervision, enlist the co-operation of provincial and municipal authorities, and advise voluntary organizations that take an active interest in the establishment of immigrants. It is the responsibility of Settlement Officers overseas to locate suitable immigrants to fill the needs ascertained and the opportunities developed by the Canadian section of the Settlement Service.[2]

R. Vineberg, *Responding to Immigrants' Settlement Needs: The Canadian Experience*, SpringerBriefs in Population Studies, DOI: 10.1007/978-94-007-2688-8_3,

The Settlement Service operated from headquarters with a single Regional Settlement Supervisor in each Province, with the exception of Ontario with four and Québec with two. The supervisors reported to the District Superintendent (equivalent to today's Regional Director General) and, until 1957, had a role roughly similar to program advisors today. There were no settlement units as such in the field. Settlement was part of the responsibilities of all immigration officers, though in practice, in larger immigration offices, some officers become specialists in counselling and placement. In 1957, a decision was taken to give line authority to the Regional Settlement Supervisors over the placement officers in the field. As the volume of work increased, Assistant Settlement Supervisors were placed under the Regional Settlement Supervisors in many locations. By 1961, the service was increasingly professional. The position of District Supervisor of Placement and Settlement was created to oversee the Regional Settlement Supervisors and their teams. In total, there were 129 full-time and 47 part-time Placement and Settlement officers across Canada.[3]

The Citizenship Branch, meanwhile, focused its activities on language training and coordination of government and non-government activities supporting the integration of immigrants. The 1951–1952 *Annual Report* noted that:

> It is a continuing policy of the Branch to encourage the co-ordination of local efforts and the establishment of joint committees to cope with the welfare, housing, educational, and social problems of newcomers and in general to promote civic and national understanding. The Branch is now working with some forty co-ordinating committees of this type, seventeen of which were formed in 1951–1952. A provincial citizenship committee was formed in Manitoba during the year.[4]

These joint co-ordinating committees carried out work very similar to the Local Immigration Partnerships being established in many parts of the country in the early twenty first century.

It took quite some time to bring the citizenship and immigration activities together. In fact, on April 15, 1954, over three years after the formation of the department, the deputy minister had to instruct the Director of Citizenship to write to the Director of Immigration to "provide you with a short statement on the functions and the activities of the Canadian Citizenship Branch."[5] It took until November 1965 before agreement was reached to coordinate the services of the two branches![6]

The post Second World War period was also the time when many new non-governmental organizations were founded to help assist, first, the displaced persons from Europe and, then, the increasing flow of immigrants. The oldest continuously operating immigrant settlement agency is the Jewish Immigrant Aid Society (JIAS), established in 1922. However, many others, including the Manitoba Interfaith Immigration Council, the Italian Immigrant Aid Society in Toronto (a forerunner of COSTI), and le Centre social d'aide aux immigrants in Montréal[7] were all founded shortly after World War II.

As the post-war economic boom took hold, it became clear that Canadian industry needed more workers, but the high cost of travel was deterring many potential immigrants. Also, Australia was offering free passage to immigrants. Therefore, the Minister of Citizenship and Immigration proposed to his Cabinet colleagues the creation of a revolving fund to provide assisted passage loans to immigrants destined to jobs deemed to be in the national interest. The fund was modest at first but grew quickly as more and more immigrants began to take advantage of the assisted passage loans.[8]

Over the years, a range of services delivered throughout the government grew up to provide some assistance to immigrants and refugees. The large movement of Hungarian refugees in 1957–1958 served to identify gaps in programming and motivated new services, including free transportation to Canada for the Hungarian refugees, and agreements with the provinces whereby the federal government assumed full responsibility for the care of refugees for the first year.[9]

In 1959, the Immigration and Citizenship section of the *Canada Year Book* featured an article on the "Integration of Postwar Immigrants" prepared by the Citizenship Branch. It is worth quoting from this at length as it provides a good summary of the official view of the settlement activities of the government and the voluntary sector:

"A primary objective of administration is satisfactory settlement. The Federal Government assists immigrants in establishing themselves in the Canadian community through the work of the Immigration Branch Settlement Service, the Canadian Citizenship and Canadian Citizenship Registration Branches and other government agencies, and cooperates closely with several voluntary agencies having the same objective....

After the War, the [Citizenship] Branch directed its attention to the great numbers of immigrants who came to this country, encouraging them to attend language classes and to prepare for Canadian citizenship; and interpreting their needs to the Canadian people, especially to the voluntary organizations that were interested in welcoming and assisting them....

The primary step in the integration process is to learn the language.... The Citizenship Branch, under arrangements with the provincial departments of education, provides free textbooks and pays 50 p.c. of the amount expended by the provinces towards the teaching costs of language classes.... They are usually evening classes held in schoolrooms during the school year.

Many voluntary organizations, immigrant aid societies and church groups also provide language instruction. Some of these classes are designed to meet the special needs of housewives, night-workers and others who are unable to attend the evening classes. They, too, receive the benefit of free textbooks as do isolated individuals who must learn the language by themselves or with the help of a tutor.

The article then went on to offer its perspective on the differences between Canadian "integration" and American "assimilation:"

In keeping with the democratic belief in the dignity and freedom of the individual, it is felt that integration should be voluntary and should not be pressed. It is assumed that integration is more moderate in its demands on the immigrant and less painful for him than assimilation would be. Assimilation usually means the complete absorption of the newcomer by the dominant culture. In the process, cultural and social differences are worn off and a more-or-less homogeneous society emerges. Integration, on the other hand, recognizes and respects the cultural contributions that may be made by people of diverse ethnic backgrounds who, nevertheless, are devoted to the welfare of the same country.

It also addressed the responsibilities of Canadians to help immigrants settle in Canada:

> The ultimate responsibility for integration rests with the Canadian people for, without their acceptance of the newcomers into community life, there can be no integration. One of the main objectives of the Citizenship Branch therefore has been to encourage understanding and co-operation between old and new Canadians and between the various ethnic groups in the population.

And, of course, the article gave due credit to the non-governmental sector as well:

> The immigrant aid societies have as their express purpose the assistance of newcomers. This they do by meeting the immigrants at the ports of entry, helping them get settled, directing them to the regular community services, and sometimes providing educational programs and special counselling services for them. Other organizations with broader community or educational aims include the integration of newcomers in their program planning. Language classes for housewives, social gatherings, program participation by newcomers, receptions following citizenship court ceremonies—these are some of the ways in which voluntary groups help the new Canadians find their place in the community. In some areas there are dozens of organizations and agencies working on behalf of newcomers. This has led to the formation of co-ordinating bodies or citizenship councils in many centres so that the work may be carried on more effectively and with less overlapping.[10]

All in all, as Canada entered the 1960s, a fairly sophisticated immigrant settlement system was being developed. However, the budgets were very small, by modern standards and, therefore, the reach of the programs was somewhat limited. In the 1958-1959 fiscal year, the Citizenship Branch expended only $248,000 on its share of language training but it also distributed 240,000 free textbooks for classes in English and 19,000 free textbooks for classes in French. The following year, some 50,000 immigrants were in language classes across the country.[11]

Meanwhile, the Settlement Service, in FY 1958–1959 made 44,800 job placements for immigrants and established 1,038 families on farms and 1,501 individuals and families in businesses. It also, as it had done for many years, "provided newly-arrived immigrants with welfare assistance during their first year in Canada if, and when, they became indigent." However, as the federal government, pursuant to the 1958 amendments to the *Unemployment Assistance Act*, was now "sharing in all direct relief assistance," it began to persuade the provinces to extend welfare services to immigrants, with the result that, in a few years, the federal government was only offering this type of support to refugees.[12]

Nevertheless, in the decade and a half, following the end of the Second World War, the concept of settlement had undergone another sea change. From its post Confederation concern of safely settling farmers on the land and then, pretty well, leaving them and their families to gradually assimilate, Canada had moved to a policy of actively encouraging integration, particularly now that most immigrants moved to urban areas. Canada and Canadians were also coming to the realization that integration was a two-way street and that Canada, as the host community, had to be accommodating to its newcomers just as they had to adjust to their new homeland.

It was also felt, within the Immigration Branch, that the Canadian model of assistance to immigrants involving the same officer corps in selection, admission and settlement was ideal. The 1964 *Admission Branch Policy Manual* stated that:

> Canada's single line of authority and control in immigration matters is unique. The visa officers abroad who select and counsel immigrants, the admitting officers at ports of entry and the officers who provide placement and settlement services at destination point are all officers of the same Branch. The result is continuous functional service to immigrants unknown in any other country. That immigration officers' duties and functions should overlap is felt to be a desirable feature as all are engaged in one task and assistance and co-operation, rather than finely drawn lines of authority, will more readily achieve the desired ends.[13]

It was also dismissive of the 'passive approach' to job placement at the National Employment Service, operated by the Department of Labour, noting that, "The key to immigration placement activities is the personal service given to the individual. An immigrant is placed in suitable employment even if this means that employers are canvassed until a job is found—we do not wait in our offices until jobs make their appearance."[14]

Unfortunately, just as the concept of integration of immigrants was evolving with such promise, its very existence was threatened.

Demise of the Settlement Service

From the very beginning of the Settlement Service's formal establishment in 1949, it had been under attack. As early as 1950, in Cabinet, Humphrey Mitchell, the Minister of Labour, expressed his view "that the operations of the Settlement Service of the Immigration Branch might duplicate functions that had heretofore been discharged and could be effectively carried on in future by the Employment Service." Walter Harris, the Minister of Citizenship and Immigration, sought to refute his colleague's claims and, "pointed out that the Settlement Service had been in existence for a long time and had operated continuously except during the war years. There were thirty settlement officers and it would be their task to perform functions in assisting immigrants which would not duplicate the work of the Employment Service. So far as employment was concerned, the Settlement Service would maintain close consultation with the Department of Labour."[15]

In 1957, the issue arose again, within the government. The Minister of Labour, Michael Starr, wrote to the Minister of Citizenship and Immigration, Ellen Fairclough, suggesting that the placement of immigrants should be the responsibility of the National Employment Service (NES). He did not receive a reply and wrote again the following year. On October 30, 1958, Minister Fairclough signed her reply to both of Minister Starr's letters and it was a long and forceful defense of the Settlement Service and its placement activities. She wrote, in part:

> Reception is one of the most important phases in the implementation of the Canadian Immigration Policy....
>
> Initial placement is an essential part of the reception of the immigrant, who is in need of services which are not generally provided to other Canadian residents through a government agency. For the first months in Canada immigrants require special assistance and guidance not only in finding employment but in locating temporary accommodation; financial assistance while awaiting employment or their first pay immediately following their arrival; arrangements have to be made with employers to make advances of salary or pay the salary weekly instead of on a semi-monthly or monthly basis; explanation of their background and training to employers; medical and dental care, etc. It is important for the immigrants to know that they have a service of the Government to turn to in time of need for they are not, like other residents in Canada, aware of the multiplicity of services made available, and it would create confusion, disappointment and hardship if upon arrival they had to consult with several of the agencies of governments in Canada....
>
> This Department is responsible for the welfare, financial need, and medical care of immigrants during the first twelve months which follow their arrival in Canada. It seems normal, therefore, that the officers of the Immigration Branch should make the necessary effort to place those who are unemployed instead of providing them with financial assistance....
>
> In summary, I am satisfied that there is no duplication between the the placement services of the Immigration Branch and the National Employment Service. The former is a vital part of our whole immigration programme and is complementary to N.E.S. placement.[16]

Three years later, in Parliament, during the 1961 debate on the department's supply, Minister Fairclough had to make a public defence of the Settlement Service in response to a question from Jack Pickersgill who, a few years earlier, as Minister of Citizenship and Immigration himself, apparently had no problems with the Settlement Service but in opposition suddenly felt that it duplicated the work of the National Employment Service.[17] This was particularly disingenuous given that while Pickersgill was minister, the Treasury Board reviewed the question of possible duplication and found that the placement "service was essential to the reception of the immigrants and should remain as a function of the Immigration Branch."[18] Jack Pickersgill was a consummate politician and never missed an opportunity to make life difficult for the other side of the House, regardless of his views on an issue.

In 1965, the federal government embarked on a major reorganization and the centre-piece of that reorganization was to create a department responsible for "manpower." This department was to include the Immigration Branch of Citizenship and Immigration while the Citizenship Program was to go to the Secretary of State Department. On December 22, 1965, OiC PC1965-2283 transferred the National Employment Service and Occupational Training Programs from the Department of Labour to the Department of Citizenship and Immigration.[19] As was normal in government reorganization, responsibilities could be changed by Order-in-Council, so the manpower service was being created within the Department of Citizenship and Immigration. However, the name change required an act of Parliament and that would follow.

On May 9, 1966, Prime Minister, Lester Pearson made a statement on the reorganization in the House of Commons. He said,

> The Government has also decided that it would be a wise course of action to place immigration under the same minister as the minister dealing with manpower generally. Immigration policy obviously must be administered in the interests of the country and of the immigrants themselves in a context that takes into account the entire position of employment, training and placement in Canada.[20]

Not everyone, however, agreed with this move. In response to the statement, Richard A. (Dick) Bell, the last Conservative minister of Citizenship and Immigration, declared that it would be a mistake to put immigration in a labour portfolio. Inevitably, he predicted, the larger, manpower part of the new department would seek to reduce immigration. He also noted that countries with separate immigration departments generally had much more vigorous immigration programs.[21] The decision also seemed to have been made without much thought as to the fate of the Settlement Service. For a brief period, the Settlement Service remained with the Immigration Division of the new Manpower and Immigration (M&I) department. Almost as an afterthought, it was decided to split the functions between the two departments. Manpower and Immigration, true to the approach described in the Prime Minister's statement, would be responsible for the economic integration of immigrants, including language training for those destined to the labour market, and the Department of the Secretary of State would be responsible for social, political and cultural integration.

The government's reorganization legislation received Royal Assent on June 16, 1966 and was brought into force on October 1, 1966. This decision marked the end of the Settlement Service because its settlement officers were not assigned to the Immigration Division but, rather, were incorporated into the Manpower Division. In the field, they were moved from Immigration Offices into the major Canada Manpower Centres. The concept of providing a unique service to immigrants was laid to rest. Instead, "the prevailing philosophy was that immigrants should turn to existing, mainstream services available to all Canadians for their settlement needs."[22] It appeared that the labour/employment forces had won their long battle against the Settlement Service. Freda Hawkins, in her account of the break-up of the Settlement Service, in her book, *Canada and Immigration, Public Policy and Public Concern*, wrote that the decision "ignored entirely the long experience of immigration officials and voluntary agencies which indicates quite clearly that, for a while at least, the immigrant is always a special case requiring, not better service, but a rather different kind of service."[23]

In reality, the Department of the Secretary of State did little or nothing in the way of providing settlement services to immigrants on or shortly after arrival. Their programs were community-based rather than focused on the individual. At the Canada Manpower Centres, officers of the former Settlement Service basically ignored a change that they thought was ill thought out and attempted to carry on as they had before, providing "all aspects of settling immigrants, looking after initial reception, counselling, accommodation, employment, and any other assistance they require when they first arrive in Canada."[24]

Nevertheless, a great deal had been lost with the demise of the Settlement Service* and there was no institutional advocate for immigrant settlement within the federal government. This created a vacuum in which there was no planning, no coordination and no initiatives. This situation would last for eight years.

Tom Kent, the Deputy Minister during the creation of Manpower and Immigration wrote, in his memoirs, that the Settlement Service "was considerably more effective than the NES, with the anomalous result that immigrants had, when they needed it, better help in finding suitable jobs than was available to unemployed citizens. This part of the immigration service was absorbed into the manpower centres. The intent was not, of course, to dilute the service to immigrants but to help in raising the quality of information and counseling available to all who needed help with employment."[25] Kent's hope that the influence of the much smaller but much more effective Settlement Service would improve the quality of the mammoth but less effective National Employment Service turned out to be a vain hope and he was one of the first to notice.

---

* As a footnote to the story of the Settlement Service, in 1954, a directive was sent to all District Superintendents and to all posts abroad noting that "the term 'Settlement Service' is still being used to describe the Settlement Division". It went on to instruct that "the phrase 'Settlement Service' must not be used as a synonym for the Settlement Division". It was feared that this might leave "the impression that Settlement Service is a function separate and apart from the responsibilities of the Immigration Branch."[26] This, like many other HQ directives, was honoured in the breach. In fact, the Settlement Division, itself, disappeared in a 1964 reorganization that placed the Settlement Service in a Canadian Service Directorate.[27]

Chapter 4
Creation of the Settlement Program

It did not take long, in bureaucratic terms, for senior management in the Department of Manpower and Immigration to recognize that the "hodge-podge" of services available to immigrants needed to be supported in a coherent manner. On March 21, 1969, Tom Kent, the Deputy Minister, wrote to his Assistant Deputy Ministers to propose striking a small task force on immigrant settlement. He wrote:

> I have had foremost in my mind for some time now the question as to whether this Department—and indeed others concerned—is properly organized to offer all the assistance which can reasonably be expected from the Federal Government to immigrants, especially those who experience settlement difficulties. This appears to be an area of concern which should receive our urgent attention, especially because of the increasing proportion of immigrants originating in areas of the world which are not traditionally source countries.
>
> What I have in mind, for example, is the situation in which we now find ourselves, where a unit of the Department which was charged specifically with immigrant settlement has been disbanded and where a fair number of relatively disjointed assistance programs are being offered (beyond the strict reception and immediate settling-in stage) not to immigrants as such, but rather to the members of the labour force. There may be a need for an effort at co-ordination of programs which themselves might be modified or strengthened to meet the particular settlement problems of immigrants. There is also the question of liaison and co-ordinating our effort with provincial authorities and private groups.[1]

As internal discussions continued, the Secretary of State Department tried to provide some "stop-gap" programming by the use of the federal government's Local Initiatives Program (LIP) to obtain project funding for some immigrant settlement projects. However, LIP project grants were short term and the settlement issue was not. The two departments negotiated proposals for a new separation of responsibilities and submitted them to their respective ministers.

Both Robert (Bob) Andras, the Minister of Manpower and Immigration, and Hugh Faulkner, the Secretary of State, realized that the time had come to address the problem and they jointly sponsored a proposal to Cabinet to create a defined Settlement Program. In the Cabinet discussion, on June 6, 1974, Mr. Faulkner,

R. Vineberg, *Responding to Immigrants' Settlement Needs: The Canadian Experience*, 27
SpringerBriefs in Population Studies, DOI: 10.1007/978-94-007-2688-8_4,
© The Author(s) 2012

proposed replacing the "economic" versus "social, political and cultural" division
of responsibility with a temporal framework. He said that under the proposed
program, "the department of Manpower and Immigration in essence would be
dealing with the short term aspects of immigrant integration through the use of its
existing services and that the Department of the Secretary of State would be
looking after the longer term aspects of immigrant integration."

Cabinet accepted the proposal and directed that:

1. a programme for providing services to immigrants be adopted; this program to be
   comprised of activities already authorized, including financial assistance for settling in,
   job counselling, placement, language and occupational training, information and
   referral services, social counselling, centers for community contact and general forums
   for immigrants' concerns;
2. responsibility in the field of services at the federal level be divided so that the
   Department of Manpower and Immigration maintains responsibility for the reception of
   immigrants and their settling into the community, including employment, accommodation, and establishing an understanding of social services available to the individual
   immigrant and his family; the Department of the Secretary of State would be
   responsible for the longer-term aspects of integration concerning the development of a
   society which is receptive to and understanding of, the needs and desires of Canada's
   immigrant community and for stimulating initiatives in the immigrant community to
   assist in its own development within a Canadian context;
3. the Department of Manpower and Immigration be responsible for the overall coordination of those voluntary organizations providing immigrant adjustment and settlement
   assistance;
4. the Department of the Secretary of State be responsible for the overall coordination of
   those voluntary organizations working to encourage greater societal understanding and
   assisting in the development of ethnic and community organizations working for the
   integration and involvement of the immigrant community in the Canadian society;
5. the Department of Manpower and Immigration and the Department of the Secretary of
   State conduct as quickly as possible a determination of those L.I.P. and other immigrant orientation projects funded by the Department of the Secretary of State to be
   continued and submit a joint proposal to the Treasury Board for the funding required;
6. efforts be undertaken to ensure that provinces accept their responsibilities for the
   provision of services to individual immigrants and the immigrant community ...[2]

The Cabinet decision, on June 6, 1974, is a formative document, not only
because it created the settlement program and broadly defined its mandate, but
because it also gave Manpower and Immigration the authority and, via the
Treasury Board, the funding to establish the what was to become the Immigrant
Settlement and Adaptation Program (ISAP) and to start to develop a close
working relationship with non-governmental organizations serving immigrants.
In consequence, in October 1974, a Settlement Branch was established, but it was
located in the Manpower Division of M&I. Nevertheless, a major step had been
taken to revitalize immigrant settlement.

In one of those coincidences of history, at the same meeting, Cabinet also had
under consideration a report on assistance to voluntary organizations and directed
that, "whenever possible, departments and agencies avail themselves of the services of Canadian voluntary organizations as a means of fulfilling their respective
mandates instead of increasing the numbers of departmental staff."[3] Therefore, the

shape of the new Settlement Program and its dependence on the voluntary sector have roots in two Cabinet decisions, both made on June 6, 1974.

Work began immediately to put in place a fully developed program. The objectives of the new branch were:

> To ensure the smooth adaptation of various categories of immigrants into the social, economic and cultural fabric of Canada according to their needs and the needs of the communities; counselling and the dispensing of information in Canada and overseas; mobilizing the services provided by the federal, provincial and municipal governments and voluntary agencies for the integration of immigrants.

It was necessary to have the program structure in place before obtaining Treasury Board authority to extend funding beyond the 51 projects, funded for a total of $810,000 in 1975/1976, that had been taken over from the Secretary of State the previous year. However, the department and Minister Andras felt that this amount was totally inadequate to provide appropriate settlement services to immigrants. He requested a further $4,190,000 for a total of $5,000,000 for contributions for the new orientation program to be called the Immigrant Settlement and Adjustment (later changed to "Adaptation") Program (ISAP). He also proposed replacing the cost-sharing agreement with the provinces for language training which cost the federal government $1,200,000 in FY1775/76 with a vastly expanded fully funded federal program worth over $14 million. Funding for the language training would come from the existing Canada Manpower Training Plan (CMTP). Finally, of course, he requested 38 additional "man-years" with 15 joining the existing six at headquarters and 23 in the regions, essentially doubling the settlement staff in the field. It should be noted that responsibility for the Adjustment Assistance Program (AAP), established in 1957, to implement the federal-provincial agreements providing that the federal government would assume the first year of the costs of refugee resettlement was also assigned to the new Settlement Branch.[4] Unfortunately, the needed funding was delayed due to the government's anti-inflation program of the late 1970s.[5]

The *Immigration Green Paper*, tabled in Parliament on February 3, 1975, served to publicize the new approach in an extensive chapter on "Services to Immigrants." The chapter also enumerated the available programs and services:

- Overseas Counselling
- Assisted Passage Loans
- Reception Services at major ports of entry
- Emergency Medical Assistance
- Interim Health Coverage, pending enrollment in provincial plans
- Family Allowance Benefits for the first year in Canada until qualified for regular benefits
- Emergency Financial Assistance
- Immigrant reception facilities at major Canada Manpower Centres
- Mobility Grants
- Occupational Training
- Language Training

Table 4.1 ISAP Program Spending 1974–1975 to 1983–1984[a]

Fiscal year	ISAP Expenditures ($)	Agencies with contracts
1974–1975	810,000	51
1975–1976	810,000	51
1976–1977	960,000	59
1977–1978	1,673,000	84
1978–1979	Not reported[b]	Not reported
1979–1980	2,173,000	Not reported
1980–1981	2,055,076	100
1981–1982	2,513,996	135
1982–1983	2,884,975	132
1983–1984	3,151,124	136

[a] M&I/E&I, *Annual Reports*, 1976-77 to 1983-84. For 1974–1975 and 1975–1976, see note 4 above

[b] *The 1978–1979 Annual Report lumped ISAP and AAP together*

The *Green Paper* also noted many limits on effectiveness including; a shortage of general counselling facilities even in major immigrant receiving communities; immigrants' lack of awareness of available services; fear of officialdom; credential recognition; under-employment; and, lack of language programs for school children, housewives [sic] and senior citizens. It also identified lack of services in immigrant languages at schools, hospitals, police forces and other emergency services. Finally, it pointed to the "disparities in the range and quality of services across the country" and observed that this did have an impact on the uneven distribution of immigrants in Canada.[6]

One of the reasons for the disparities in service was that the small (ISAP) budget, inherited from Secretary of State, was devoted largely to contracts to agencies in Montréal, Toronto and Vancouver. Expansion to other cities would require more money and that would be a long time in coming. The Annual Reports of the department showed the slow grow of ISAP, in its first decade, reflected in Table 4.1.

Improvements to the Settlement Program

The creation of the ISAP program was an immediate response to the lack of proper counselling services. And over the next several years the structure of three programs for all immigrants and an additional program for refugees took shape. A CIC discussion paper from 2001 concisely summarizes the development of the three key programs of the Settlement Program:

In 1974, grants to nongovernmental organizations (NGOs) were initiated under the new Immigrant Settlement and Adaptation Program (ISAP)...

Prior to 1990, language training was provided under the auspices first of the Adult Occupational Training (AOT) Act of 1967, and subsequently, the National Training Act of 1982. This legislation permitted adult immigrants destined to the labour market to obtain training in one of Canada's official languages. In 1986, the Settlement Language Training Program (SLTP) was introduced as a pilot program. SLTP funded nongovernmental organizations to provide up to 500 h of basic language training to adults not destined to the labour market, primarily immigrant women. This program was designed mainly to provide language skills that would assist immigrants in coping with everyday life. SLTP was made permanent in 1989. Approximately 10% of the national budget for language training was allocated to SLTP, and 90% was allocated to labour market oriented language training. Language programs were delivered for the most part through the direct purchase of seats in provincially approved institutions.

Additionally, the Host Program was launched as a pilot project in March of 1984. It was originally designed to further enhance the settlement process of government assisted refugees and designated persons who qualified for support under the then Adjustment Assistance Program (AAP), now known as the Refugee [sic] Assistance Program (RAP).[7]

The Resettlement Assistance Program (RAP), that replaced AAP in 1998, is a program for refugees, who are, essentially, sponsored by the Canadian government through the Government Assisted Refugee category. RAP provides them with reception on arrival in Canada, temporary housing in reception houses, initial orientation to Canada, assistance in locating permanent accommodation, income support for the first year in Canada and referral, as required, to other settlement services. This work is carried out by some two dozen RAP service providers across Canada. The modern program rationale developed from discussions at a Symposium on Refugee Sponsorship in 1984, attended by sponsors as well as representatives from non-governmental organizations, church groups, and federal and provincial governments. However, the original Adjustment Assistance Program began in 1957 to honour the federal government's commitment to care for Hungarian refugees for a full year following their arrival in Canada.

The program had been the responsibility of the Settlement Branch, when it was part of the Manpower Division, but shortly after its move to the Immigration Division (see Chap. 6–*Repatriation of the Settlement Program*), a new Refugee Branch was created and it was transferred to that branch. RAP continues to be administered by the Refugees Branch at CIC national headquarters but it is delivered by settlement units in CIC regional and local offices, along with the settlement programs under the purview of CIC's Integration Branch. The Adjustment Assistance Program (AAP) was administered and delivered solely by immigration staff. However, in 1998, when the program was re-designated as RAP, CIC became the 'program manager' and all services, except income support, are now delivered by service provider organizations (SPOs).

In the seventies, the Settlement Program was faced with responding to a number of refugee movements. In August 1972, President Idi Amin of Uganda ordered all residents of Asian ancestry to leave Uganda. This was the first major refugee movement of non-Europeans that Canada responded to. The following year, the Pinochet coup d'état in Chile created a Chilean refugee movement as well. The relatively large number of refugees arriving in a short period of time, for the first time since the Czech uprising in 1968, placed pressure on the new program but also brought about increased funding for it. These movements, however, were on a small scale compared to the refugee crisis of Indochinese "Boat People", millions of whom fled Vietnam, Laos and Cambodia in the wake of the reunification of Vietnam following the long war between the North and the South. Canada accepted over 100,000 Indochinese refugees, most of whom were chosen in an innovative plan whereby the federal government undertook to sponsor the same number of refugees as did private groups and organizations under the Private Sponsorship of Refugees (PSR) Program. Quickly, there developed a need for far more language teachers, occupational trainers and counsellors for the refugees. This was a period of growth in the program, both in terms of finance and in terms of expertise. Settlement service agencies were established in almost every city of any size throughout Canada. Many of the service provider organizations in operation today can trace their roots to the late seventies or early eighties and to responding to the needs of the "Boat People."

Organizational Challenges

In the 1974 Cabinet decision to create the Settlement Program, there still lay a challenge that had been identified by a Cabinet member. During the Cabinet discussion, Stanley Haidasz, the Minister of State for Multiculturalism, expressed a concern that coordination of the various programs in two departments with three ministers (including himself) directed at the very same client group–immigrants– might prove difficult. He stated his view that "there should be one and not three Ministers responsible for immigrant integration."[8] He was right, but it was to be many years before this came to be.

Notwithstanding the Cabinet decision, within the Department of Manpower and Immigration, immigrant settlement was still perceived to be more closely tied to the Manpower side of the department than to the Immigration side, so the Settlement Program remained within the Manpower Division. In the field, Immigrant Counselling and Placement Units (ICPU) had been established in the main Canada Manpower Centres (CMCs) in Montreal, Toronto, Winnipeg, Calgary and Vancouver. The concept was that after initial counselling and placement, from an ICPU counsellor, immigrants would then quickly switch over to normal Canada Manpower Centre services.[9] And, as can be seen from the list of ICPU locations, many large cities, including Ottawa, did not have any dedicated immigrant counsellors at their CMC.

In locations where there were no dedicated settlement units, the type and quality of the immigrant counseling at that time was compromised in that manpower counsellors' performance assessments were based, in large part, on the number of clients served. Even the most dedicated manpower counsellors could not provide the intensive and time-consuming counselling required by immigrants unless they were willing to sacrifice their career in doing so.[10]

Chapter 5
Constitutional Issues and Settlement in Québec

The evolution of federal-provincial relations in Canada has had an enormous impact on immigration in general and, in this respect, settlement is no exception. Immigration and settlement with it were key elements in the constitutional discussions in the 1980s and 1990s.

The Meech Lake Accord

In 1984, Brian Mulroney's Progressive Conservatives defeated the Liberals and formed a Government committed to "bringing Québec into the Constitution." To that end, Mulroney commenced constitutional discussions that led to the Meech Lake Accord. An element of Québec's constitutional propositions, presented to the federal government on May 15, 1985, included the proposal that:

> The Constitution should enlarge upon the Cullen-Couture Agreement of 1978 by confirming the paramountcy of Québec's powers in the matter of selection, and by extending that paramountcy to the integration and settlement of immigrants.[1]

The constitutional negotiations ultimately resulted in the Meech Lake Accord on June 3, 1987. The Meech Lake Accord included the "constitutionalization" of Federal-Provincial Immigration Agreements, in particular the Cullen-Couture Accord, at the time, the most recent of a series of Canada-Québec agreements on immigration. Sections 2 and 3 of the Meech Lake Accord provided that:

> 2. The Government of Canada will, as soon as possible, conclude an agreement with the Government of Québec that would
>
>   (a) incorporate the principles of the Cullen-Couture agreement on the selection abroad and in Canada of independent immigrants, visitors for medical treatment, students and temporary workers, and on the selection of refugees abroad and economic criteria for family reunification and assisted relatives,

R. Vineberg, *Responding to Immigrants' Settlement Needs: The Canadian Experience*,
SpringerBriefs in Population Studies, DOI: 10.1007/978-94-007-2688-8_5,
© The Author(s) 2012

(b) guarantee that Québec will receive a number of immigrants, including refugees, within the annual total established by the federal government for all of Canada proportionate to its share of the population of Canada, with the right to exceed that figure by five per cent for demographic reasons, and

(c) provide an undertaking by Canada to withdraw services (except citizenship services) for the reception and integration (including linguistic and cultural) of all foreign nationals wishing to settle in Québec where services are to be provided by Québec, with such withdrawal to be accompanied by reasonable compensation, and the Government of Canada and the Government of Québec will take the necessary steps to give the agreement the force of law under the proposed amendment relating to such agreements.

3. Nothing in the Accord should be construed as preventing the negotiation of similar agreements with other provinces relating to immigration and the temporary admission of aliens.[2]

The Accord required the approval of the Parliament of Canada and the legislatures of all provinces by June 23, 1990. As the Manitoba and Newfoundland legislatures did not approve it by the deadline, the accord failed.[3]

The Charlottetown Accord

A second round of constitutional negotiations began immediately and resulted in the Charlottetown Accord. Section 27 of that accord provided that:

27. Immigration
    A new provision should be added to the constitution committing the Government of Canada to negotiate agreements with the provinces relating to immigration.
    The Constitution should oblige the federal government to negotiate and conclude within a reasonable time an immigration agreement at the request of any province. A government negotiating an agreement should be accorded equality of treatment in relation to any government which has already concluded an agreement, taking into account different needs and circumstances.[4]

The Charlottetown Accord also failed, this time in a national referendum on October 26, 1992 in which it was rejected by six provinces and the Yukon.[5] The *Constitution Act* requires that at least two-thirds (seven) of the provinces representing 50% of the Canadian population approve this type of constitutional amendment.

The Canada-Québec Immigration Accord

The federal government and the Province of Québec had been in the process of negotiating a new immigration agreement even before the Meech Lake Accord negotiations were taking place. Therefore, in the wake of the failure of Meech

Lake, the federal government did not await the outcome of further constitutional negotiations to move on the Meech commitment to conclude a new immigration agreement with Québec, incorporating the principles of the Cullen-Couture agreement. The result is the current *Canada-Québec Accord Relating to Immigration and Temporary Admission of Aliens*, signed on February 5, 1991 by federal Minister of Employment and Immigration, Barbara McDougall and Québec Minister of Cultural Communities and Immigration, Monique Gagnon-Tremblay. It came into force on April 1, 1991.[6]

Québec had already established a network of *Centres d'orientation et formation des immigrants (COFI)*, that provided initial orientation and counselling to immigrants destined to that province. The province was eager to take on full responsibility for immigrant settlement in Québec. They achieved this aim with the 1991 agreement.

The 1991 Canada-Québec Accord is very similar to the Cullen-Couture Accord but it did include a number of important changes respecting settlement. Section 2 contains a new objective:

> 2. An objective of this Accord is among other things, the preservation of Québec's demographic importance within Canada and the integration of immigrants to that province in a manner that respects the distinct identity of Québec.

Furthermore, Québec's wish to assume responsibility for settlement was confirmed in sections 24 and 25:

> 24. Canada undertakes to withdraw from the services to be provided by Québec for the reception and the linguistic and cultural integration of permanent residents in Québec.
> 25. Canada undertakes to withdraw from specialized economic integration services to be provided by Québec to permanent residents in Québec.

Annex B of the Accord sets out the compensation to be paid to Québec for the provision of settlement services to immigrants in Québec. The formula is controversial because it provides for a continual increase in payments to Québec according to a complicated formula based both on government spending generally and on increases (but not decreases) to the number of immigrants destined to Québec. Therefore, the compensation under the Accord increases even if immigration to Québec does not.[7] The effect has been that transfers to Québec under the accord have increased from $75 million in 1991–1992[8] to $258.4 million in 2011–2012.[9] This rapid increase in federal immigration transfers to Québec in comparison to spending in the rest of Canada would lead to complaints from other provinces. (See Chap. 8 below, *Solving the Funding Issues*). Furthermore, the transfer of authority over immigrant settlement to one province opened the possibility that other provinces might also be interested in administering immigrant settlement programs.

Chapter 6
Repatriation of the Settlement Program

The *Federal Immigrant Integration Strategy* was launched in the context of the new five-year *Immigration Plan for* 1991–1995 presented to Parliament in the fall of 1990. The government expected that immigration levels would be the focus of the cross-Canada consultations that were undertaken. However, the question of integration of newcomers to Canada quickly took centre-stage. While there was widespread support for immigration across Canada, the support was contingent on the existence of effective programs to help immigrants integrate into Canadian society. While the focus of government settlement assistance, since the creation of Manpower and Immigration (later Employment and Immigration) Canada, had been labour market integration, many of those consulted felt that settlement programs needed to ensure that newcomers to Canada could participate fully in the social and cultural as well as the economic life of Canada.

In response, the *Strategy* introduced a broader view of immigrant integration than had been envisaged before. It was designed facilitate "the full participation of immigrants in all aspects of Canadian life. The strategy coordinates the efforts of several federal departments, and encourages a renewed partnership with the provinces, the private sector and local community groups in meeting immigrant needs".[1] More funding was promised for language training over the life of the five-year plan and an ambitious target was set to increase the proportion of immigrants receiving language training from 28% in 1990 to 45% in 1995.[2] The two separate language programs were merged and eligibility was broadened to include all adult immigrants on an equal basis regardless of whether or not they were destined for the labour market. Also, the new program, introduced in 1992, was renamed as the Language Instruction for Newcomers to Canada (LINC) program to emphasize the larger target group. The Host Program was made permanent and expanded to include immigrants as well as refugees. Eligibility for service providers to deliver the ISAP program was extended across a broader range of community organizations and non-profit groups in order to provide enriched services to a broader immigrant base. Finally, reception services at major ports of entry points were

R. Vineberg, *Responding to Immigrants' Settlement Needs: The Canadian Experience*,   39
SpringerBriefs in Population Studies, DOI: 10.1007/978-94-007-2688-8_6,
© The Author(s) 2012

introduced as pilot-projects and later made permanent. Funding was increased but not nearly enough to respond to the demand for the broadened service platform.

The *Federal Immigration Integration Strategy*, in deeming not only the economic outcomes but the social, cultural and political integration of immigrants to be essential, created the bureaucratic environment necessary to justify the unification of the various elements of the settlement program within Canada Immigration. The government's recognition of this broader view of integration implied that integration is a long-term process that begins when immigrant first applies, or a refugee is first selected, to come to Canada, and it continues until and even after he or she acquires citizenship. Finally, it acknowledged that communities must play their part and that integration is a two-way street that requires accommodation and adjustment by both the immigrant and the receiving community.[3]

So, in 1992, the settlement programs within the Employment Sector of Employment and Immigration Canada (CEIC) were moved to the Immigration Sector. In practical terms, this meant that the Immigrant Counselling and Placement Units in major Canada Employment Centres (CECs) across Canada were moved to the Canada Immigration Centres in those cities and reconstituted as Settlement Units. At national headquarters, staff were also moved and the Settlement Branch was placed under the Associate Deputy Minister, Immigration, at CEIC. Settlement staff, across the country, were happy with the decision. They too had observed the evolving needs of their clientele and supported the focus moving to more language training and more support in the process of integration. They felt the Immigration Sector would be more supportive of these aims.[4]

The Employment Sector of CEIC, continued to fund and deliver the Labour Market Language Training (LMLT) program that offered advanced language training intended to prepare skilled immigrants for the workplace and, of course, it also continued to offer its occupational training programs to immigrants along with Canadians. Settlement staff retained contacts with their CEC colleagues and accessed occupational training for their clients with relative ease.

The remarriage of Settlement and Immigration faced a temporary separation the following year. On June 25, 1993, Kim Campbell was sworn in as Prime Minister and immediately announced a government reorganization that included the creation of a Department of Public Security that would include immigration but not immigrant settlement. The Settlement Branch was to be moved to the new Department of Human Resources and Labour. After reuniting with immigration after a 26-year absence, it was a body blow to settlement staff across Canada to be told they would be returning to the "employment" ministry.

Thankfully, the new exile was short-lived. On October 25, 1993, the Campbell government was defeated by Jean Crétien's Liberals and, when the new cabinet was sworn in on November 4, it included a Minister of Citizenship and Immigration. Shortly after, in the company of new minister, Sergio Marchi, Associate Deputy Minister, Ian Glen, announced to Settlement Branch staff that they and their colleagues in the field would be part of the new department to be known as Citizenship and Immigration Canada (CIC). His announcement was met with resounding cheers.[5] In the new department, settlement and citizenship were grouped within a new Integration Branch, thus bringing settlement and citizenship back together as well.

The new Liberal government launched nation-wide consultations on future directions for immigration in the winter of 1994. As was the case in the previous government's consultations, settlement issues again took centre-stage. Stakeholders, particularly in those cities receiving large numbers of immigrants and refugees, were concerned with duplication and overlap of services. A festering issue was that federal settlement funding only applied to permanent residents but in Vancouver, Montreal and, particularly, Toronto, there were large numbers of refugee claimants whose needs had to be met by the municipalities. CIC was expected to address these concerns.

Chapter 7
Program Review and Settlement Renewal

Trying to Give it Away

In early 1995, the federal government looked at the increasing pressures on settlement budgets and the complexity of settlement delivery and decided that a new approach was needed. As had already been done with Québec, the government was considering devolving the administration of settlement programs, either to provinces (as with Québec) or to other bodies. David Neuman, National Director of Settlement Renewal, bluntly told the Standing Committee on Citizenship and Immigration:

> the Department of Citizenship and Immigration has decided to withdraw from the direct administration of settlement services and funds. What that means is the federal government will continue to provide funding for immigrant settlement services, but it will no longer be directly involved in the administration of those funds or in the delivery of those services."[1]

Mr. Neuman went on to say, however, that CIC was "looking at the enduring federal role and national principles."[2] The department's *Outlook on Program Expenditures and Priorities* put it somewhat more tactfully:

> We will be working closely with provincial and local organizations to find ways to respond more effectively to the settlement and integration needs of communities and to ensure that appropriate services are provided by those best positioned to do so…. Together with our partners, we will develop mechanisms to identify local settlement service priorities and appropriate funding to meet such priority needs. This will also involve moving the delivery mechanisms to regional and local levels. Full transition to this new approach will take two to three years.[3]

Within the non-governmental settlement sector, the prospect of devolution caused serious concerns regarding the standards of services available across the country. The experience with the devolution to Québec was not considered a positive model, because funding was transferred as a grant and the province was

R. Vineberg, *Responding to Immigrants' Settlement Needs: The Canadian Experience*,
SpringerBriefs in Population Studies, DOI: 10.1007/978-94-007-2688-8_7,
© The Author(s) 2012

under no obligation to use all the funding for immigration and did not do so until 2009. At the same time, there was a clear consensus that there was an enduring federal role in settlement services that included working with partners to define and uphold national principles, so the settlement sector hoped that federal leadership would continue in some form.[4]

Settlement Renewal was an idea that came out of the federal government's "Program Review" exercise, in 1995–1996, designed to address the large federal deficit that existed at that time. In Program Review,

> Ministers were asked to review their own portfolios and provide their view on the federal government's future roles and responsibilities. Government programs and activities were reviewed using six tests: serving the public interest; necessity of government involvement; appropriate federal role; scope for public sector/private sector partnerships; scope for increased efficiency; and affordability.[5]

Citizenship and Immigration had to absorb some $62 million in budget cuts and it proposed turning over administration of the Settlement Program to provinces that wished to take it on, the rationale being that Settlement Program efficiencies could be gained as provinces deliver social services and education. In reality, another factor was taken into consideration. Of the major programs delivered by CIC (admissions, ports of entry, enforcement, citizenship and settlement), which could be devolved with the least damage to the essential operations of the department? In the context of the times, a program that had only been with the immigration program for a few years seemed the most expendable.

Consultations and Negotiations

CIC held two rounds of nationwide public and federal-provincial consultations on Settlement Renewal in 1995 and 1996. Their purpose was to convince as many stakeholders as possible of the wisdom of the approach and as many provinces as possible to take on delivery of settlement programs, the federal government, of course, transferring the budget for that province. The first round of consultations, from November 1995 to January 1996, addressed the key issues that had been raised by stakeholders and the provinces when the Settlement Renewal initiative had first been made public.

Those issues were:

1. Shared Principles—What should be the basis of the agreements between CIC and new delivery partners?
2. Accountability—How can a system be designed to improve flexibility and responsiveness to regional requirements and still provide appropriate accountability for the expenditure of funds voted by Parliament?
3. Humanitarian Commitments—What services are required to meet the needs of resettled refugees and how can Canada's international commitments be met in the absence of a federal delivery system?

4. Enduring Federal Role—What should be CIC's role beyond that of providing funding?
5. New Ways to Administer—What models could be adopted at the regional or local level to streamline program delivery while ensuring better co-ordination and local input to determine service priorities?

The second round of consultation, from May to July 1996 was to inform stakeholders of the results of the first round. The consultations indicated that:

- settlement should be based on common principles across Canada, including community responsibility to help the adjustment process;
- accountability was necessary but that reporting requirements should be simplified;
- refugee resettlement assistance was likely better left with the federal government;
- the federal enduring role should include involvement in priority setting, encouragement of more research on integration and a return to offering counselling to immigrants prior to departure for Canada; and,
- the provinces were really the only entities, other than the federal government, with the capacity to deliver settlement program administration effectively.

The Standing Committee on Citizenship and Immigration also held its own hearings on Settlement Renewal and released its report in June 1996. It was supportive of the initiative but recommended expanding settlement funding to a five-year period following arrival regardless of the citizenship status of the recipient of services. It did not want new citizens to be penalized for taking out Canadian citizenship by losing access to settlement programs. However, the reality of the time was that settlement funding was inadequate even for the needs of the newly arrived immigrants and such a move would take resources away from the most in need, namely recently arrived immigrants and refugees.

The provinces, while welcoming many of the proposals, were not happy with the level of settlement funding which, except in Québec, had remained the same for several years and several provinces also did not feel that the regional allocation of existing funding was equitable. In the context of Program Review, in fact, they feared there would be cutbacks to federal funding. This concern was addressed, to a degree, by the imposition of the Right of Landing Fee that would raise sufficient funds to maintain the funding levels within the federal immigration fiscal framework. This resulted in the federal government offering to increase spending outside Québec from its base of $118.4 million by $62.3 million to a total of $180.7 million. The new funds, ironically, almost exactly the same amount CIC was expected to save from its operating budget in Program Review, were made available in 1997–1998.[6]

The new funding persuaded Manitoba and British Columbia (BC) to conclude "Settlement Realignment" agreements in 1998. As a result, the following year, both provinces began delivering settlement services.[7] CIC was not able to conclude settlement realignment agreements with any other provinces and, therefore, the avowed aim of withdrawing from direct administration of the settlement program was not achieved, much to the relief of the settlement community in those other provinces. Accordingly, in 1999, the Minister "decided not to actively seek new agreements with the provinces."[8]

There was much trepidation in Manitoba and British Columbia as those provinces took over administration of settlement. In Manitoba, the settlement community soon saw that the province was going to continue and, indeed, enhance settlement programs and initial concerns faded quickly. In fact, the Manitoba Immigrant Integration Program (MIIP) has introduced innovative programs, such as its 'Entry Program', a three week full-time introduction to Canada and Manitoba. Offered to all immigrants on arrival in Manitoba, it provides orientation and incorporates language training at the level of competence of the immigrant. Furthermore, Manitoba reported on its expenditures in an open and transparent way. However, in British Columbia, the settlement community was dismayed by the fact that a large proportion of the funds transferred from CIC was "administered under 'general revenues', allocated to community colleges and welfare-based skills training, with uncertain service accessibility and outcomes for eligible immigrants."[9] In recent years, the BC government has allocated an increasingly higher proportion of the funding received from the federal government to the BC Settlement and Adaptation Program (BCSAP) which delivers programs similar to LINC, ISAP and Host.

Implications of Program Review at Human Resources

The approach to Program Review by the Department of Human Resources Development (HRDC) also created challenges for the Settlement Program. Even following the transfer of the program to Immigration, in 1992, there was a close working relationship between settlement officers and human resources officers in order to ensure rapid placement of immigrants into occupational training courses. However, included in its contribution to Program Review, HRDC proposed that labour market training be devolved to the provinces. And, unlike the Settlement Program, the labour market programs were well funded and the provinces generally were eager to take on these programs. Therefore HRDC quickly concluded agreements with most provinces.

The transfer of these programs to the provinces, combined with recent changes to Employment Insurance (EI) legislation that limited employment assistance, including training, to those who were eligible for employment insurance by virtue of previous work and EI contributions, effectively eliminated newly arrived immigrants' access to occupational training. Furthermore, HRDC cancelled the LMLT program in 1996, eliminating federal advanced language training for immigrants.

The Settlement Allocation Model

Another issue that came to the fore, with the transfer of settlement funding to British Columbia and Manitoba, was the question of how to divide the funding fairly. This had always been an issue, but it was an internal issue, fought out between national headquarters and the regional offices of the department. However, now with the provinces of British Columbia and Manitoba administering the settlement program, they were determined to receive their fair share of funding. So, inherent in the settlement devolution plan, there had to be a settlement allocation model as the amount of funds available was limited. The model was based on the three year rolling average of the number of immigrants destined to each province (outside Québec) and it also provided an additional weighting based on the anticipated amount of language training required for immigrants destined to particular provinces. All provinces argued that it did not account adequately for the demands of refugees, whose settlement needs are greater than the average immigrant, and smaller provinces also felt that a base amount was required so that jurisdictions with few immigrants would receive an amount adequate to establish basic services. The model was modified to account for these concerns, though not necessarily to the extent desired.

As it is, necessarily, retrospective, provinces with a rapidly growing immigrant movement have tended to be frustrated by their allocations based on the "distant past." However, the formula now provides a cushion should immigration to a province decline. Indeed, the annual decrease is limited to 10% per year in recognition that settlement serving agencies need time to adjust to smaller budgets.

Chapter 8
Solving the Funding Issues

The Canada-Ontario Immigration Agreement

Many provincial governments watched with dismay as settlement funding to Québec increased annually and, after 1997, the funding in other provinces remained the same. Ontario, which received the most immigrants, led the chorus of complaint. Ontario Premier Dalton McGuinty fiercely denounced "the unfairness that had seen our province receive 57% of new immigrants but only 34% of national funding." Ontario officials calculated that Ontario was receiving $819 per immigrant for settlement services whereas Québec received $3,806 per immigrant.[1] In 2005, with a federal general election approaching, Paul Martin's Liberal government authorised CIC to put sufficient funding on the table to conclude the first ever immigration agreement with Ontario, on November 21, 2005.[2] The crucial funding arrangements are found in Section 8 of the agreement:

> 8.1 Beyond the annual settlement funding currently allocated in Ontario, in the order of $109.6 M in 2004–2005, Canada agrees to invest additional resources for settlement services and language training for prospective immigrants to, and immigrants residing in Ontario. Canada commits to providing incremental funding that will grow over a five-year period to reach a cumulative total of $920 M in new investments by 2009–2010. For planning purposes, this incremental funding is projected to be disbursed in accordance with the following profile:

> 2005–2006—$50 M;
> 2006–2007—$115 M;
> 2007–2008—$185 M;
> 2008–2009—$250 M;
> 2009–2010—$320 M.[3]

The enormous increase in settlement funding was welcomed in Ontario. In fact, the new challenge was how to effectively spend the new money which, by 2009–2010, represented a four-fold increase in five years from $110 to 430 M.

R. Vineberg, *Responding to Immigrants' Settlement Needs: The Canadian Experience*,
SpringerBriefs in Population Studies, DOI: 10.1007/978-94-007-2688-8_8,
© The Author(s) 2012

Other Provinces Catch Up

The big increase in Ontario funding was not immediately matched in the eight other provinces. Therefore, the Ontario deal incited anger among the other provinces, British Columbia and Alberta in particular. Provinces other than Ontario and Québec had long pointed to the disparity in settlement funding as a reason immigrants were less likely to settle elsewhere. When the Conservative government was elected in January 2006, with Prime Minister Stephen Harper being from Alberta, Ed Stelmach, then Alberta Minister of International and Intergovernmental Affairs, was quick to state that Alberta wanted the new federal government to address immigration programs and deal with issues about the per capita funding of immigrant settlement programs.[4] Wally Oppal, the BC Minister responsible for immigration also indicated that his province wanted to negotiate a similar funding deal to that of Ontario.[5] The lobbying for equal funding resulted in the 2006 federal budget allocating a $77 million increase in settlement funding outside of Québec in order to redress the funding disparity.[6] However, this amount only partly addressed the disparity and in 2008–2009, a further $121.6 million were directed to the other provinces to create a rough parity among all provinces.[7]

When the *Canada-Ontario Immigration Agreement* (*COIA*) expired in 2010, the federal government decided that settlement funding to Ontario would be combined with that of all other provinces and allocated on the same basis. In December 2010, CIC announced settlement funding for 2011–2012. In 2010, CIC had been subject to a 'Strategic Review' by central agencies and the department had to identify savings of 5% of its budget. As settlement funding is, by far, the largest budget item, the savings had to be found there. Overall settlement funding, outside Québec, was reduced by over $50 M (from $652 M in 2010–2011 to $599 M in 2011–2012). Since immigration to Ontario and British Columbia had declined over the previous five years and had increased sharply on the Prairies, funding to Ontario and BC was reduced by $44 and 8 M respectively while it increased on the Prairies by $12 M.[8] Nevertheless, at roughly $600 M, settlement funding was more than three times greater than it had been some six years earlier. The major beneficiaries, of course, have been new immigrants who have far greater access to immigrant settlement programs, especially language training, across the country.

As a result of the *Canada-Québec Accord*, settlement realignment agreements with BC and Manitoba, and the *Canada-Ontario Immigration Agreement* (*COIA*), settlement services are delivered in different ways across Canada. In Québec all settlement services including refugee resettlement assistance is provided solely by the province; in BC and Manitoba all settlement services, except the Resettlement Assistance Program, are delivered by the province. In Ontario, COIA requires formal consultation with the province before settlement funds are expended by CIC and in Saskatchewan, the Atlantic Provinces and in the territories, informal consultations take place regularly but the ultimate decisions on CIC settlement funds are made exclusively by CIC. Of the provinces where CIC delivers settlement services, it is only in Alberta that a cooperative management approach has

Fig. 8.1 A modern refugee reception centre: welcome place in Winnipeg, nearing completion, 2011, Robert Vineberg, courtesy, Manitoba Interfaith Immigration Council

been adopted and is reflected in a formal *Statement of Understanding Regarding Settlement Programs and Services for Immigrants in Alberta.* This statement provides that CIC and Alberta Employment and Immigration will consult jointly with Albertans on settlement priorities, jointly consider proposals from settlement service providers and decide on funding shares. In this way, service providers need only make one proposal and will find out how much funding they will receive and from whom in a reasonably seamless process. This approach could well be a model for other provinces in the post-Settlement Renewal era.

Resettlement Assistance Program

Unfortunately, the vast increase in settlement funding did not apply to one key element of settlement programming, namely the Resettlement Assistance Program. This program provides key services uniquely designed to support Canada's Government Assisted Refugees (GARs) program, under which some 7,500 Convention refugees are sponsored, annually, by the Canadian government. As noted earlier, these services include, providing them with reception on arrival in Canada, temporary housing in reception houses, initial orientation to Canada, assistance in locating permanent accommodation, income support for the first year in Canada and referral, as required, to other settlement services. The RAP funding remained at $45 million, the level established in 1998 when the current program design was adopted. Inflation and expenses associated with a higher proportion of 'high needs' refugees being selected overseas eroded the RAP budget. The RAP program is funded separately from other settlement services and, therefore, did not

Fig. 8.2 Welcome Place, Winnipeg, Manitoba: an apartment for refugees, 2011, Robert Vineberg, courtesy, Manitoba Interfaith Immigration Council

Fig. 8.3 Welcome Place, Winnipeg, Manitoba: a common room, 2011, Robert Vineberg, courtesy, Manitoba Interfaith Immigration Council

benefit when the government increased settlement funding during the 2005–2008 period. This constant budget at a time of rising costs put tremendous strain on RAP service providers who were struggling to work within clearly inadequate budgets.

Finally, in 2010, the RAP under-funding was addressed when about $9 million was added to the RAP budget, representing a 20% increase over 1998 funding levels.[9] This will serve to meet current program requirements but will not allow program enhancements such as providing additional specialized counselling and orientation to GARs and allowing them to stay longer in refugee reception houses while receiving the enhanced orientation programming Figs. 8.1, 8.2 and 8.3.

Chapter 9
Foreign Credential Recognition

"It must be recognized that the value to Canada of the skilled immigrant depends in part on how he [or she] is received. Some professional associations, trade unions and provincial licensing authorities are not as ready as they might be to recognize qualifications earned in another country. Consequently some immigrants are not able to follow their own occupation on arrival here and must accept alternative employment at least until they are able to meet the applicable Canadian standards.... It must be hoped that this problem will be overcome as the leaders of public opinion come to recognize the economic advantage of more mobility, particularly among professional people and skilled workers, both nationally and internationally...."[1]

When almost all of Canada's skilled workers came from the United States, the United Kingdom or Western Europe, the recognition of their credentials was not a big issue. This changed in the 1960s, as Canada opened her doors to immigrants from all parts of the world. Soon after, many of our skilled immigrants were arriving in Canada not knowing if their credentials would be recognized. The issue is not new and the quotation above is not new. It comes from the Federal Immigration Policy *White Paper* of 1966. Unfortunately, the situation described in the *White Paper*, over 40 years ago, still exists.

Multiple jurisdictions, outdated attitudes towards foreign credentials, and lack of information—both among Canadians about the strengths and weaknesses of foreign academic institutions and among prospective immigrants about their realistic chances of having credentials accepted in Canada have been perennial obstacles to immigrants' success in Canada. Clearly, all immigrants do not possess credentials that ought to be recognized in Canada. Some simply do not make the grade. However, when immigrants can make the grade, it is an incredible waste not only for them but for Canada as well.

After years of federal provincial meetings and false starts, progress started to be made in the context of internal trade barriers. The *Agreement on Internal Trade* (*AIT*), signed on July 18, 1994 and effective on July 1, 1995 committed the federal, provincial and territorial governments to move forward on many fronts to improve internal trade and one of these was labour mobility. Chapter 7 of the agreement

R. Vineberg, *Responding to Immigrants' Settlement Needs: The Canadian Experience*,   55
SpringerBriefs in Population Studies, DOI: 10.1007/978-94-007-2688-8_9,
© The Author(s) 2012

has, as its purpose, "to enable any worker qualified for an occupation in the territory of a Party to be granted access to employment opportunities in that occupation in the territory of any other Party."[2] In this context, the AIT provided a forum to discuss the issue of foreign credential recognition, not only for immigrants but for Canadians who obtained credentials abroad. In October 1999, the AIT sponsored a conference entitled "Shaping the Future: Qualification Recognition in the twenty first century". This national conference, with over 500 delegates, noted that while the AIT deals with recognizing the qualifications of workers from other provinces and territories, regulators are often asked to consider the qualifications of workers from other countries. This was the first time since the signing of the AIT that regulatory bodies and other interested parties jointly discussed interprovincial labour mobility and foreign credential recognition at the same time.[3] The Forum of Labour Market Ministers (FLMM) that had been tasked to implement the Labour Market provisions of the agreement subsequently decided that it was within their purview "to help ensure that fully licensed workers with foreign training enjoy mobility within Canada, comparable to Canadian-trained workers."[4] They established a Labour Market Coordinating Group (LMCG) to carry on this work. In 2005, the LMCG reported that it "has worked to promote recognition practices so that skilled workers–trained either in Canada or abroad–can enjoy the same mobility once they are qualified in one Canadian jurisdiction."[5] Work continued slowly leading to a significant step forward in 2009.

On November 30, 2009 the federal government, provinces and territories agreed to a *Pan-Canadian Framework for the Assessment and Recognition of Foreign Qualifications*. It is intended to be the long awaited breakthrough that will start to make credential recognition faster and easier. The stated goal of the Framework is to "articulate a new, joint vision for governments to take concerted action to improve the integration of immigrants and other internationally-trained workers into the Canadian labour market."[6]

The *Framework* is merely a statement and is not a legal document. However, it is the first government commitment to improve qualification assessment and recognition practices across Canada. The *Framework* commits governments to develop a fair, transparent, timely and consistent qualification recognition process. The fairness criteria will be crucial to the success or failure of the system. They are:

• Standards must be objective, reasonable and bias-free;
• Methods for assessment must be not only necessary but also sufficient for determining whether occupational standards are met;
• Canadians and internationally-trained applicants must be treated equally respecting requirements to be met;
• Assessment results have to include a clear explanation for the decision;
• Assessment processes must be efficient and avoid duplication, particularly where multiple assessments are required by different authorities.

In order for this to work for those whose credentials are not recognized, skills upgrading has to be available if they are close to meeting requirements and guidance on employment in related occupations has to be in place if they have no chance of qualifying.

Timeliness is also crucial. The stated goal of rendering decisions within one year of application will be a vast improvement over most situations that exist today.

Priority was to be placed on regulated occupations and this is appropriate because this is where the biggest obstacles lie. The first goal was to implement the *Framework* for Architects, Engineers, Financial Auditors and Accountants, Medical Laboratory Technologists, Occupational Therapists, Pharmacists, Physiotherapists and Registered Nurses by December 31, 2010. By December 2012, a second group of occupations consisting of Dentists, Engineering Technicians, Licensed Practical Nurses, Medical Radiation Technologists, Physicians and Teachers (K − 12) is to be added.[7]

Governments cannot do this alone. They have to obtain the cooperation of regulatory bodies to make the assessment process work, and that of universities and colleges, to provide specialized courses for skills upgrading. Also, in the absence of public scrutiny, there is no guarantee that things will change. Governments have agreed to report annually on progress. For far too long, many skilled immigrants who have chosen Canada arrived in Canada to find that Canadian institutions chose to ignore the contribution they wanted to make to this country. It appears that, finally, the first step to resolving this colossal waste of talent has been taken.

The federal government has also been working on providing better information to foreign trained skilled workers and professionals on Canadian requirements and how to navigate the often complex process involving over 400 licensing bodies across Canada. In 2003–2004, the government committed $68 million over six years to a Foreign Credential Recognition (FCR) Program. This resulted in the establishment of a "Foreign Credential Recognition Office", initially at Human Resources but transferred to CIC in 2007 and re-designated as the "Foreign Credential Referral Office" (FCRO) in acknowledgement of the fact that recognition lies with licencing bodies, most of which are provincial creations. Therefore, the role of the FCRO lies in providing up-to-date and accurate information, path finding and referral services. It does so by means of an interactive website linked to almost all licencing bodies in Canada and offers in person service through the over 300 Service Canada offices. The FCR also funds a pilot project to provide in person counselling to prospective immigrants in the Federal Skilled Workers stream prior to departure for Canada. The Canadian Immigration Integration Project (CIIP) is administered by the Association of Canadian Community Colleges and operates in Guangzhou, China, New Delhi, India and Manila, Philippines and London, England. A key element of the counselling is to provide information on credential recognition.[8] The FCR was extended by two years with an additional $50 M in funding in 2009.[9]

Much remains to be done in order to assure that the qualifications and credentials of immigrants in Canada are given proper recognition, but after decades of handwringing, progress is now taking place on several fronts and the hope, expressed in the 1966 *White Paper*, may soon be finally realized.

Chapter 10
Emerging Issues and the New Terms and Conditions

Francophone Immigration Outside Québec

The CIC-Francophone Minority Community Steering Committee was established by CIC and the Fédération des communautés francophones et acadienne in March 2002 to facilitate the selection, reception and integration of newcomers in Francophone minority communities outside Québec. This initiative received broader support with the March 2003 launch of the Government's *Plan d'action pour les langues officielles*. This Action Plan came with funding, of which $9M over five years was allocated to CIC.[1] In September 2006, in Saint Boniface, the francophone sector of Winnipeg, the CIC-Francophone Minority Community Steering Committee released its Strategic Plan and the improvement of settlement services dedicated to francophone immigrants was a major element of the strategy.[2]

The key lesson from this exercise for the Settlement Program was indentifying the need for stand-alone francophone settlement services, as opposed to French-language capacity in predominantly English-speaking settlement agencies. As a result CIC regions used the funding from the Official Languages Program as well as regular contribution funding to establish francophone reception centres in major cities across Canada. Often, these facilities were housed within existing francophone institutions which have been able to provide administrative and, sometimes, financial support. British Columbia and Manitoba also provide support for their Francophone communities. Furthermore, in Winnipeg, CIC has contracted with the Francophone Welcome Centre to deliver the RAP program for the growing number of Francophone refugees destined to Winnipeg.

While concern was expressed by some that these reception centres were too expensive, given the relatively small number of francophone immigrants, it is generally realized that without settlement facilities in place in advance, one cannot expect francophone immigrants to choose locations outside Québec.

R. Vineberg, *Responding to Immigrants' Settlement Needs: The Canadian Experience*, SpringerBriefs in Population Studies, DOI: 10.1007/978-94-007-2688-8_10, © The Author(s) 2012

Settlement Services Abroad

The major role of immigration foreign service officers is to make proper selection decisions so that only qualified immigrants and legitimate refugees are admitted to Canada. However, another major responsibility had been to counsel immigrants on their move to Canada—what to expect; how to prepare; credential recognition, the Canadian way of life and so on. This did take place until the early 1990s, when administrative changes in the overseas immigration program resulted in most immigrants being evaluated without being seen in person. While this did result in some efficiencies in processing, settlement professionals, as well as immigrants and refugees themselves, soon were complaining that newcomers were sorely lacking in accurate information about Canada.

In order to address this emerging problem, the Canadian Orientation Abroad (COA) initiative was implemented in 1998. Its purpose is to provide orientation sessions abroad to assist refugees and immigrants destined to Canada to prepare for their move and to begin, abroad, the process of facilitating their integration into Canadian society. The COA is currently delivered on behalf of CIC by the International Organization for Migration (IOM), under a contribution agreement.

COA sessions are offered to all classes of immigrants and refugees who have been selected for permanent resident status. However, priority is given to Convention refugees (CRs). In addition, the participation of women and children is a priority so that they and their spouses or fathers can begin to understand that women and children have inherent rights in Canada.[3] In 2009, the IOM delivered COA sessions from permanent sites in Colombia, Egypt, Ethiopia, Ghana, Jordan, Kenya, Lebanon, Nepal, Pakistan, Philippines, Russia, Sri Lanka, Sudan and Syria. From the inception of the program until March 2009, the COA provided sessions to over 124,000 people.[4]

Similarly, the Canadian Immigrant Integration Program (CIIP), an orientation program for federal skilled workers and their families was established as a small pilot project in 2007, operated on behalf of CIC by the Association of Canadian Community Colleges. Originally to be a two year pilot, given its early successes the pilot was extended until November 2010.[5] By providing skilled worker immigrants information on life and work in Canada prior to arrival in Canada, it was hoped that immigrants would more quickly establish themselves in appropriate employment. During the life of the pilot project, over 9,000 people completed the program.[6] The evaluation of the pilot determined that, to a great extent, the program has been effective.[7] As a result the CIIP has been funded as an ongoing program for a further three years (2010–2013) and now has four offices abroad, in China, India, Philippines and the United Kingdom. CIIP is now available to Provincial Nominees as well. CIIP offers orientation programs in these countries and undertakes visits to surrounding countries as well.[8]

Enhanced Language Training

In 2004 CIC, in recognition that LINC as general language training, could not meet the advanced language needs of professionals hoping to enter the labour-market, introduced the *Enhanced Language Training (ELT)* program. This began to address the problem created in 1996 when Human Resources cancelled the Labour Market Language Training program. The initiative combined employment-specific language training with Occupational training, mentoring, internships, placements and other work-related experiences. This combination of learning was designed to prepare skilled immigrants for jobs in the Canadian labour market commensurate with their skills and qualifications. The program was launched on the basis of a 50/50 partnership with each province. However, most provinces did not have funding available and this ratio was lowered and eventually eliminated. However, in provinces, such as Alberta, which did enter into a full partnership, the additional funding meant that more programming could be undertaken. This program has now been integrated into the general settlement program.

Welcoming Communities Initiative

In March 2005, the federal government announced *A Canada for All: Canada's Action Plan Against Racism.* It provided $56M over five years, some of which was allocated to CIC. This funding allowed CIC to develop the Welcoming Communities Initiative (WCI). The WCI is quite broad in concept but it focused on programs in communities and schools to help the general population understand and appreciate immigration and race issues and, in doing so, reduce racism, discrimination and ethnic conflict in Canadian communities. Prior to the change in Settlement Program Terms and Conditions (see below), CIC could not use general settlement funds in this way.

The Welcoming Communities Initiative focused on an expansion of the Host Program and the development of the Settlement Workers in School (SWIS) initiative. The settlement needs of young people are unique and have, until recently, been largely unaddressed by federal settlement programs. However, the anti-racism funding, referred to above, provided an opening for CIC to start developing programs for young people and to respond to pleas from settlement serving agencies who had identified the need long ago. The SWIS initiative, that provides funding to locate settlement counsellors in schools, has been of particular help to immigrant students and their families when trying to navigate the Canadian educational system. The in school settlement workers also help the school administration and teaching staff to work more effectively with immigrant young people.

The *Action Plan Against Racism* had been a program of the Canadian Heritage Department but was transferred to CIC in 2008 when the government moved the Multiculturalism Program from Heritage to CIC (see below).

Local Immigration Partnerships

A promising initiative that came out of the *Canada–Ontario Immigration Agreement* and is now spreading across the country is the establishment of Local Immigration Partnerships (LIPs). In 2008, CIC, in co-operation with the Ontario Ministry of Citizenship and Immigration issued a Call for Proposals to establish LIPs in several Ontario communities. The purpose of the LIPs is to, "provide a collaborative framework for, and facilitate the development and implementation of, sustainable local and regional solutions for successful integration of immigrants… LIPs seek to help communities put immigration on their overall planning agenda…" Indeed, some communities had created partnership councils on their own initiative.[9]

The LIPs promise to improve co-ordination of services to immigrants by bringing together all those who should be involved in the settlement and integration process at the local level. As noted earlier, they are very much a reincarnation of the joint co-ordinating committees that existed in the 1950s and 1960s.

Contribution Accountability Framework

The Settlement Accountability Framework, as it was called at the time, was introduced in 1999 to ensure accountability of settlement and resettlement program expenditures through the monitoring of service delivery and the evaluation of program effectiveness and efficiency. There were five major elements to the framework:

• Performance measurement (through iCAMS—the Immigration Contribution Accountability Measurement System);
• Program evaluation;
• The contribution agreement process (assessment, negotiation, management, project monitoring and evaluation);
• Provincial-territorial accountability (reporting by British Columbia and Manitoba); and,
• The Management Control Framework (MCF).

At the time iCAMS, the electronic reporting system had many "bugs" and met lots of resistance, especially from larger organizations who had their own accountability systems and now had to input data into two separate systems. A failing of all the accountability systems is that Québec is not included as its funding is in the form of a grant, so no accountability provisions are involved. Furthermore, although Manitoba and B.C. have to meet accountability provisions, the settlement service providers in those provinces are not required to input data into iCAMS therefore resulting in challenges in comparing and evaluating the information provided against that provided in the other provinces.

Nevertheless, given the enormous scale of modern settlement funding, adequate accountability throughout the settlement system is a fundamental requirement.

New Terms and Conditions

In 2008, the Treasury Board approved CIC's proposal to introduce a modernized settlement approach that consolidated settlement programming that had formerly been compartmentalized into the three longstanding programs (ISAP, LINC and Host) as well as more recent programs such as ELT, into a comprehensive outcomes-based program. The new single program organizes services into three general client oriented themes:

1. information and orientation;
2. language and skills; and,
3. labour market access.

It also provides for activities in support of community connections; support services; and needs assessment. An Accountability, Risk and Audit Framework was developed at the same time to reflect the modernized approach to the settlement program, including the revised terms and conditions for settlement funding, an improved structure for policy and program development and service delivery, and an enhanced accountability structure for achieving and reporting on results.

The new Terms and Conditions will allow much more flexibility in order to fund innovative settlement programming. In addition, funding can now be directed to some categories of prospective immigrants, in particular to fund orientation programs abroad. Finally, it also allows a significant proportion of funding to be used for capital projects.[10]

The Transfer of the Multiculturalism Program to CIC

On October 30, 2008, the Government approved OiC, PC 2008–1732 transferring

> control and supervision over portions of the Department of Canadian Heritage relating to multiculturalism to the DEPARTMENT OF CITIZENSHIP AND IMMIGRATION, and (b) certain powers, duties and functions in relation to multiculturalism to the MINISTER OF CITIZENSHIP AND IMMIGRATION.[11]

The transfer of the Multiculturalism portfolio from the Department of Canadian Heritage to CIC should provide new opportunities for improving coordination between the immigration, citizenship, and multiculturalism programs. In particular, this should result in a seamless interface between relatively short-term settlement programs and longer-term integration programs that promote inclusion, participation, and shared citizenship.[12]

And, with this decision, for the first time since 1966, there is, now, one federal minister responsible for all major aspects of immigrant integration.

Chapter 11
Summary and Conclusion

It is hard to imagine what life might be for an immigrant or refugee arriving in the Canada of the twenty first century and not being able to receive counselling and assistance or language training. Nor is it conceivable that Canada would select refugees abroad and not look after their initial housing and welfare needs. Indeed, settlement services are now seen as an integral part of Canada's immigration program and as an integral part of ensuring the success of immigrants to Canada. The Settlement Program of 2011 is vastly different from the program of 1891 or even 1991 but it retains the same goal: the successful establishment of newcomers in Canada. Over the years, the approach has changed greatly, moving from one focused on protecting British North American residents and, thereby, incidentally helping immigrants, to the new Canadian nation's focus on moving newcomers safely to the land they were settling and, providing after-care, and, finally, to the postwar concept of active integration of immigrants into an accommodating host population.

We, in Canada, can certainly learn from our own settlement experience and, indeed, while no other immigrant receiving country can simply emulate Canada's settlement program, the lessons drawn from Canada's experience can certainly serve to inform and benefit other countries and individuals and organizations in those countries who are still struggling with settlement policy, programs and practices. In terms of overall philosophy, we have found that:

- Settlement services that were often initiated to protect the resident Canadian population were quickly transformed into efforts designed to retain the immigrants who chose to come to Canada.
- No immigration program can be considered comprehensive without a vibrant and viable settlement element.
- Settlement and integration is a two-way street. The best settlement program will fail in the absence of a welcoming community. This is a lesson that Canada has learned, and then forgotten, only to rediscover again, several times through its history.

R. Vineberg, *Responding to Immigrants' Settlement Needs: The Canadian Experience*, 65
SpringerBriefs in Population Studies, DOI: 10.1007/978-94-007-2688-8_11,
© The Author(s) 2012

- Governments, therefore, need to develop a strategy for immigration and settlement and promulgate it to the public.
- In a federal state, such as Canada, settlement and integration will inevitably involve both levels of government. Indeed, even in unitary states, regions and municipalities have an essential role to play. Cooperation and coordination are difficult but remain essential to the success of any settlement program.
- Settlement and integration are 'whole of government' activities. While a strong lead department is necessary, all government departments need to craft policies in support of their government's settlement programs.
- In a country, such as Canada, with two major linguistic and/or cultural groups, settlement programs must be available to encourage integration into both of the groups.

Over the years, there have been many significant lessons, developments, innovations and failures in Canada's settlement program. The following are worth highlighting:

- Immigration must benefit the entire country and a proper network of settlement services needs to be in place. Canada was very good at this in the late nineteenth century and early twentieth century. In the latter half of the twentieth century we concentrated settlement services in a few major cities and were surprised that immigrants did not wish to go elsewhere. It was only at the turn of the twenty first century, in developing a regionalization effort, that we rediscovered the need to provide settlement services where we want immigrants to locate.
- Immigrants need to feel welcome and the earlier (even before arriving in Canada) we can deliver this message and offer useful services, the more successful immigrants will be.
- Offering intensive orientation and language training to immigrants on arrival, is the best way to increase successful integration. Settlement delayed is settlement denied.
- Immigrants and refugees are not like other residents. While, like residents, they all require common services from government, immigrants arrive with the disadvantage of not understanding the host culture, not having a support network and not knowing how best to navigate the bureaucratic labyrinth. Settlement services are required to facilitate and accelerate the integration process.
- Settlement occurs everywhere. Settlement workers need to be located in schools and libraries and hospitals. And all residents need to be willing to step forward and offer help when necessary.
- Canada has still work to do in addressing the issue of recognition of foreign credentials but by dedicating substantial resources to the issue, Canada is making progress. Obstacles to integration have to be identified and addressed.
- Occupational training is as necessary, if not more necessary, for immigrants as for long-time residents. In abandoning dedicated programs and funding for immigrant labour market training, Canada took a big step backwards and we are only now beginning to repair the damage.

- Canada's decision to encourage non-governmental organizations to deliver settlement services was a brilliant way to involve communities and to stretch resources by means of community volunteer networks supporting settlement professionals.
- A welcoming country is composed of welcoming communities and, indeed, welcoming individuals and families. A program, such as Canada's Host program, can be very effective in encouraging integration at a very basic human level.
- Acceptance that diversity and immigrant integration cannot be separated. Anti-racism programming is a necessary component of an effective settlement program.
- Well constructed settlement programs are often expensive and those spending public funds need to be accountable for how the money is spent and for the outcomes of the programs offered. This is essential, both to the integrity of programs but also to maintaining general public support for these programs.
- Integration takes a long time. Both immigrants and the host community must be prepared to make a long-term commitment to settlement and integration.
- Immigration and settlement planning go hand in hand. Any government program worth doing is worth funding adequately. Governments ought not to increase intake of immigrants without following through with properly funded settlement services.

Canada's immigrant settlement experience demonstrates that, even in a country such as Canada, which is quite advanced in its immigration settlement programs, this field of endeavour remains a work in progress. Therefore, on the basis of the historical perspective provided by this book, we can identify some research areas that might have a positive impact on further developments in settlement policy, programs and practice. These might include:

- Comparison studies of settlement success in jurisdictions that offer or do not offer intensive orientation programs before and/or on arrival.
- Given that settlement and integration takes place over time, more longitudinal studies of particular areas of immigrant settlement (for example, integration in a number of comparable smaller communities) are required.
- Comparative approaches to qualification recognition by licensing bodies in order identify both best practices and systemic barriers.
- Studies of the benefits of occupational training programs, including internships with Canadian employers, in order to determine how such programs need to be tailored to immigrant needs.
- Studies of orientation programs offered prior to arrival to determine their effectiveness and to identify other subjects that could be included, such as initial language training.
- Studies comparing settlement outcomes in different jurisdictions within Canada, such as provinces or cities of similar size.
- Studies of areas of federal-provincial disagreement and how they have been resolved (or not).
- Histories of the older settlement serving organizations.
- Comparative studies of the Canadian settlement experience with that of other immigrant receiving countries

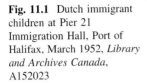

Fig. 11.1 Dutch immigrant
children at Pier 21
Immigration Hall, Port of
Halifax, March 1952, *Library
and Archives Canada*,
A152023

And, of course, I could not conclude without encouraging fellow historians to research and write about specific aspects of Canada's immigrant settlement experience. There is a wealth of information that has been barely touched upon. This book is an attempt to begin to fill this gap in Canada's historiography, but it is only a start. Too often, we have repeated the mistakes of the past or have abandoned the successful practices due to a simple lack of knowledge of our past (Fig. 11.1).

This story began with Lord Durham's admonition that governments who encourage immigration must be prepared to secure "every possible facility and assistance" in support of their successful settlement. This vision of an ideal settlement system is far closer to reality in today's Canada than when Durham wrote those words almost two centuries ago. However, neither Canada nor any other country has yet achieved this ideal. There is still much more that could be done to ease the path of integration for newcomers in Canada or in any other country. I hope, having made it to the end, that the reader will feel better placed to influence the future of immigrant settlement whether in Canada or elsewhere.

Appendix 1
Canadian Immigration Halls

As with so many aspects of our history, Canadians have simply been very poor in remembering and preserving our immigration history. Across the country, but particularly in the west, the Immigration Service operated an extensive system of 'immigration halls' to provide temporary shelter for immigrants, on arrival and en route to their destinations. Originally called 'immigration sheds,' as in other countries, the more impressive term 'immigration hall' was adopted later and became the common usage by the 1890s.

The immigration hall became, very much, the tangible symbol of Canada's commitment to its immigrants in the late nineteenth and early twentieth centuries. The concept of truly providing for the immigrant rather than just "getting them out of the way" was a key element in the government's thinking. Even before Confederation, in order to provide basic comfort and care to arriving immigrants and to protect them from the countless hustlers trying to part immigrants and their life savings, the government of the Province of Canada decided that immigration stations consisting, not only of offices for immigration agents, but also of decent accommodation for immigrants ought to be provided. These had been built, both at ports of arrival such as Québec City and Montreal, and also at inland points, including Ottawa, Kingston, Toronto and Hamilton. And, in 1872, the government of the new Dominion of Canada authorized the construction of two more stations, in London, Ontario, and in the capital of its newest province, Winnipeg, Manitoba.[1]

It was a clear signal of the importance the Canadian government attached to populating the west that, once Canada had purchased the Northwest Territories from the Hudson's Bay Company, one of the first federal public works in the new territory was to build an immigration shed at the Forks of the Red and Assiniboine Rivers, in what is now Winnipeg, within steps of the location of present local

---

[1] LAC. *OiC, PC1872-0062B,* June 21, 1872.

R. Vineberg, *Responding to Immigrants' Settlement Needs: The Canadian Experience,*   69
SpringerBriefs in Population Studies, DOI: 10.1007/978-94-007-2688-8,
© The Author(s) 2012

Citizenship and Immigration Centre and Prairies regional office. The immigrant shed could hold 250 immigrants at a time, while arrangements were made to move them onward to their homesteads, first by Red River Cart and later by train. This shed was found not to be sufficient and a second shed was added at the Forks the following year doubling the capacity to 500.[2]

With the arrival of the Canadian Pacific Railway (CPR) mainline in 1881, immigrants began arriving in Winnipeg by train in greater and greater numbers, so a new and larger immigration hall had to be built near the new CPR station at Main St., beside the CPR mainline. The first hall in the area of the CPR line was constructed in 1881. It was replaced, successively, by two other wooden immigration halls, the second of which, built in 1890, was much larger, designed to accommodate the growing numbers of immigrants passing through Winnipeg.[3] Elsewhere, across the Prairies, smaller immigration halls sprouted wherever they proved necessary. By the early 1900s there was a standard three story wood-frame design for immigration halls and most new halls were built to that standard design.

However, in Winnipeg, through which all immigrant trains from the East passed, a much larger facility was required. In 1906, a grand brick and stone immigration hall opened beside the CPR Station.[4] The 1890 hall was also retained, to accommodate 'foreign'—that is not British—immigrants. British and American immigrants got to stay in the new hall, which offered about 100 rooms for families and single women in addition to dormitories for single men. The new hall was designed for 500 people but, in a pinch, could accommodate twice that number. By 1911, there were about 50 immigration halls across the country, mostly on the Prairies.[5] In that year, the Minister of the Interior, Frank Oliver, explained, in Parliament, the purpose of immigration halls:

> ...another very important part is that of dealing with the immigrants after they arrive in Canada. ...it is our policy to facilitate, as far as possible, the immigrant reaching the destination and the purpose for which he came to Canada. For that reason, we have a system in the western provinces of distributing immigrants on the land. There is what might be called a central distribution office in Winnipeg in charge of the Commissioner of Immigration. All railroads of the west radiate from Winnipeg, and at different points throughout the western provinces which immigrants are likely to seek, we have immigration halls, that is, places, where immigrants may be temporarily entertained on leaving the train and before they go out on the land.[6]

In order to accommodate the growing numbers passing through Winnipeg, by 1928, there were three immigration halls in operation—two by the CPR station

---

[2] Rodger Guinn. *The Red Assiniboine Junction: A Land Use and Structural Study 1770–1980*, (Manuscript Report No. 355). (Ottawa: Parks Canada, 1980), 108–110 *passim*.

[3] *Henderson Directories* for Manitoba, 1881–1900.

[4] Ivan J., Saunders, R.R.Rostecki, and Selwyn Carrington. *Early Buildings in Winnipeg, Vol. III* (Ottawa: Parks Canada, 1974–77), 76, 77.

[5] "Bruce Walker Autocrat of Canada's Immigrants," *New York Times*, October 15, 1910.

[6] Canada, HoC. *Debates 1910–11*, 5170, 5171.

and one near the Canadian National Railway (CNR) Station. According to the 1928–29 *Annual Report* of the Department of Immigration and Colonization, the three halls in Winnipeg accommodated over 20,000 people during that fiscal year, with the average stay being four to five days.[7] In the twenties, as settlement was mostly in northern areas of the Prairies, halls in cities such as Brandon and Regina were closed, but the hall in Edmonton operated as a secondary distribution point for immigrants heading to the areas to the north, such as the Peace River country and smaller halls were in communities such as Prince Albert, North Battleford, Athabaska, Peace River and Grand Prairie. In fact, a new hall was built in Edmonton just at the beginning of the 1930s, too late for the immigration boom and just in time for the bust of the Great Depression.

In addition to the halls in the Prairies, halls operated in major eastern cities and at the ports of Vancouver, Québec and Halifax. Pier 21, in Halifax, included temporary accommodations and functioned as an immigration hall for many years. During both world wars, the halls were often used as barracks or veterans' hospitals and in the postwar period, demobilization centres for returning soldiers. Following the Second World War, the halls also received thousands of war brides, en route to their new homes in Canada, prior to reverting to their original use once large-scale immigration resumed. The Hungarian refugee crisis was the last time that the halls were used on a major scale and, as more and more immigrants chose to travel by air, rather than by sea and by rail, the need for the halls waned. The last halls were closed in the 1960s. The grand hall in Winnipeg continued as the Prairies regional office until 1966 and as a local immigration office until 1969. Unfortunately, it was torn down in 1975.[8]

Only a handful of immigration halls survive, including the halls in Halifax (Pier 21), in Edmonton, in Prince Albert and in North Battleford. In Edmonton, after lying vacant for over a quarter century, the immigration hall has recently been renovated as transitional inner city housing. Appropriately, the building still retains its old name: 'Immigration Hall.'

---

[7] Minister of Immigration and Colonization. *Annual Report, 1927–28* (Ottawa: King's Printer, 1929), 95.

[8] Winnipeg *Tribune*, March 13, 1975, cited in Ivan J Saunders, R.R.Rostecki,and Selwyn Carrington, *Early Buildings in Winnipeg, Vol. III* (Ottawa: Parks Canada, 1974–77), 79. For more information on immigration halls in Winnipeg, see Robert Vineberg, "Welcoming Immigrants at the Gateway to Canada's West: Immigration Halls in Winnipeg, 1872–1975," *Manitoba History*, No. 65 (Winter 2011), 13–22.

Bibliography

Abbreviations

AIT	Agreement on Internal Trade
CIC	Citizenship and Immigration Canada (1994–present)
C&I	Department of Citizenship and Immigration (1950–1966)
CYB	Canada Year Book
E&I	Canada Employment and Immigration Commission (1978–1994)
FCRO	Foreign Credential Recognition Office
FLMM	Forum of Labour Market Ministers
HoC	House of Commons
LAC	Library and Archives Canada
M&I	Department of Manpower and Immigration (1966–1978)
OiC	Order in Council
PC	Privy Council
PCO	Privy Council Office
RSC	Revised Statutes of Canada
SCCI	House of Commons Standing Committee on Immigration

Primary Sources

Documentary

AIT. *The Agreement on Internal Trade*. Winnipeg: Internal Trade Secretariat, 2010. http://www.ait-aci.ca/index_en/ait.htm (accessed April 9, 2011).

Canada, *RSC 1976–77 c. 52: An Act Respecting Immigration to Canada*.

R. Vineberg, *Responding to Immigrants' Settlement Needs: The Canadian Experience*,   73
SpringerBriefs in Population Studies, DOI: 10.1007/978-94-007-2688-8,
© The Author(s) 2012

Canada, *The Provincial Statutes of Canada*.

CIC – *Settlement Policy Files*.

CIC – *Federal-Provincial/Territorial Agreements*, http://www.cic.gc.ca/english/department/laws-policy/agreements/index.asp (accessed April 9, 2011).

C&I – *Immigration Policy Manual*, Ottawa 1964 – unpublished, numbered binder.

Craig, Gerald E, editor, *Lord Durham's Report, An Abridgement of the Report on the Affairs of British North America* (Toronto and Montreal: McClelland and Stewart, 1963) 126.

HoC, *Debates*.

LAC, RG2, Privy Council Office. *Cabinet Conclusions 1946–1976*, available at http://www.collectionscanada.gc.ca/databases/conclusions/index-e.html, (accessed April 9, 2011).

LAC, RG2. Privy Council Office. Series A-1-a, *Orders-in-Council*.

LAC, RG76. - *Immigration Records*.

Lower Canada. *Provincial Statutes of Lower Canada*.

M&I, Minister of. *Canadian Immigration Policy—White Paper on Immigration*, Ottawa: Information Canada, 1966.

New Brunswick. *The Statutes of the Province of New Brunswick*.

Nova Scotia. *The Statutes of the Province of Nova Scotia*.

RSC 1976-77 c. 52. *An Act Respecting Immigration to Canada*.

RSC 2001, c. 27. *Immigration and Refugee Protection Act*, http://laws.justice.gc.ca/eng/I-2.5/index.html (accessed April 9, 2011).

Upper Canada. *The Statutes of Upper Canada*.

Interviews

Glen, D. Ian, Former Assistant Deputy Minister, Immigration Operations, Canada Employment and Immigration Commission and former Associate Deputy Minister, Citizenship and Immigration Canada - January 6, 2010.

Crawford, James (Jim) R., Former Supervisor, Immigration Counselling and Placement Unit, CEC Winnipeg and Supervisor, Settlement Unit, CIC Winnipeg – January 10, 2010.

Secondary Sources

Government

AIT – *Annual Reports*—http://www.ait-aci.ca/index_en/reports.htm (accessed April 9, 2011).

Canada. Special Joint Committee of the Senate and of the House of Commons on Immigration Policy, *Report to Parliament.* Ottawa: Information Canada, 1975.

Canadian Heritage, Department of. *A Canada For All: Canada's Action Plan Against Racism.* Ottawa: Public Works and Government Services, 2005.

CIC. *Consultations on Settlement Renewal, Round II, Finding a New Direction for Newcomer Integration.* Ottawa: 1996.

CIC. *Departmental Outlook on Program Expenditures and Priorities, 1995–96 to 1997–98.* Ottawa: 1995.

CIC. *Departmental Performance Report*, period ending March 31, 2009, Ottawa: Public Works and Government Services, Ottawa: 2009.

CIC. Foreign Credentials Referral Office, *Progress Report 2007–08,* http://www.credentials.gc.ca/about/progress-report2007.asp (accessed April 9, 2011).

CIC. *Immigrant Integration in Canada: Policy Objectives, Program Delivery and Challenges*, a draft for discussion. Ottawa: Integration Branch, CIC, 2001.

CIC. *Report on the Evaluation of the Delivery of the Canadian Orientation Abroad Initiative*, http://www.cic.gc.ca/EnGLish/resources/evaluation/orientation.asp (accessed April 9, 2011).

CIC, Integration Branch. *Settlement Program, Implementation of the Modernized Approach*, PowerPoint presentation, 2009.

C&I. *Annual Reports 1949–50 to 1965–66.* Ottawa: King's Printer/Queen's Printer, 1950–1966.

C&I. *Canadian Immigration—An outline of developments in the post-war period, Reference Paper No. 1.* Ottawa: Queen's Printer 1958.

C&I. "Developments in Canadian Immigration." In Dominion Bureau of Statistics, *Canada Year Book, 1957–58*, 154–176. Ottawa: Queen's Printer, 1958.

C&I. "Integration of Postwar Immigrants," In Dominion Bureau of Statistics, *Canada Year Book, 1959*, 176–178. Queen's Printer, Ottawa, 1959

Department of Agriculture. *Annual Reports, 1867 to 1892*. Ottawa: Queen's Printer, 1868–1893.

Department of Immigration and Colonization. *Annual Reports 1918–19 to 1930–31*. Ottawa: King's Printer, 1919–1931.

Department of the Interior. Annual Reports, 1892 to 1917, Ottawa: Queen's Printer/King's Printer, 1893–1918.

Economic Council of Canada. *New Faces in the Crowd—Economic and Social Impacts of Immigration.* Ottawa: Economic Council, 1991.

E&I. *Annual Reports,* 1977–78 to 1993–94. Ottawa: 1978–1994.

E&I. *Annual Report to Parliament: Immigration Plan for 1991–1995.* Ottawa: 1990.

E&I. *Annual Report to Parliament, Immigration Plan for 1991–1995, Year Two.* Ottawa: 1991.

Government of Canada. *The Next Act: New Momentum For Canada's Linguistic Duality—The Action Plan For Official Languages.* Ottawa: 2003.

Great Britain, Committee on the Survey of the Coasts, &c. of Scotland. *First Report-Emigration,* House of Commons, Reports, Vol. IV, Paper No. 80, London:1803.

Internal Trade Secretariat, *AIT Annual Reports 1999–2000 to 2009–2010.* Winnipeg: Internal Trade Secretariat, 2000–2010. AIT annual reports are available at http://www.ait-aci.ca/index_en/reports.htm (accessed December 10, 2009).

M&I. *Annual Reports,* 1967–68 to 1976–7. Ottawa: 1968–1977.

M&I. *Immigration Policy Perspectives,* Volume 1 of the Report of the Canadian Immigration and Population Study. Ottawa: Information Canada, 1974.

M&I. *The Immigration Program,* Volume 2 of the Report of the Canadian Immigration and Population Study. Ottawa: Information Canada: 1974.

Special Joint Committee of the Senate and of the House of Commons on Immigration Policy. *Report to Parliament,* Ottawa: 1975.

Statistics Canada. *Canada Year Book Historical Collection,* http://www65.statcan.gc.ca/acyb_r000-eng.htm (accessed April 9, 2011).

Non-Government

Abella, Irving and Troper, Harold. *None Is Too Many, Canada and the Jews of Europe 1933–1948*, Toronto: Lester & Orpen Denys, 1986.

Choquette, Leslie, "Recruitment of French Emigrants to Canada 1600-1760." In *To Make America—European Emigration in the Early Modern Period*, edited by Ida Altman and James Horn, 131–171. Berkeley and Los Angeles: University of California Press, 1991.

Becklumb, Penny. *Immigration: The Canada-Quebec Accord, BP-252E*. Ottawa: Library of Parliament, Law and Government Division, Parliamentary Research Branch, 2008.

Biles, John; Burstein, Meyer and Frideres, James, ed., *Immigration and Integration in Canada in the Twenty-first Century*. Montreal and Kingston: McGill-Queen's University Press, 2008.

Comité directeur Citoyenneté et Immigration Canada - Communautés francophones en situation minoritaire, *Plan stratégique pour favoriser l'immigration au sein des communautés francophones en situation minoritaire*, Ottawa: 2006.

Corbett, David C. *Canada's Immigration Policy*. Toronto: University of Toronto Press, 1957.

Cowan, Helen I. *British Emigration to British North America, The First Hundred Years*. Toronto: University of Toronto Press, 1961.

Cowan, Helen I. *British Immigration before Confederation*, Historical Booklet 22. Ottawa: Canadian Historical Association, 1978.

Dirks, Gerald E. *Controversy and Complexity—Canadian Immigration Policy during the 1980s*. Montreal and Kingston: McGill-Queen's University Press, 1995.

Hawkins, Freda. *Canada and Immigration, Public Policy and Public Concern*. Montreal and London: McGill-Queen's University Press, 1972.

Hawkins, Freda. *Critical Years in Immigration—Canada and Australia Compared* 2nd ed. Montreal and Kingston: McGill-Queen's University Press, 1991.

Kelley, Ninette and Trebilcock, Michael. *The Making of the Mosaic—A History of Canadian Immigration Policy*. Toronto: University of Toronto Press, 1998.

Kent, Tom. *A Public Purpose, An Experience of Liberal Opposition and Canadian Government*. Kingston and Montreal: McGill-Queen's University Press, 1988.

Knowles, Valerie. *Forging our Legacy—Canadian Citizenship and Immigration, 1900-1977,* (commissioned by Citizenship and Immigration Canada). Ottawa: Public Works and Government Services, 2000.

Knowles, Valerie. *Strangers at our Gates—Canadian Immigration and Immigration Policy, 1540-2006, revised edition.* Toronto: Dundurn Press, 2006.

Johnson, Stanley C. *A History of Emigration From the United Kingdom to North America 1763–1912.* New York: Augustus M. Kelley, 1966 (reprint of 1913 original).

Johnston, H. J. M. (1972). *British Emigration Policy 1815–1830 'Shovelling out Paupers'.* Oxford: Clarendon Press, 1972.

Macdonald, Norman. *Canada, 1763–1841 Immigration and Settlement.* Toronto: Longmans, Green and Co., 1939.

Macdonald, Norman. *Canada-Immigration and Colonization 1841–1903.* Toronto: Macmillan of Canada, 1966.

Saunders, Ivan J., R. R. Rostecki, and Selwyn Carrington. *Early Buildings in Winnipeg, Vol. III.* Ottawa: Parks Canada, 1974–77.

Seigfried, André. *Canada,* London: Jonathon Cape, 1937.

Smith, W. G. (1920). *A Study in Canadian Immigration.* Toronto: Ryerson Press, 1920.

Vineberg, Robert. "Federal-Provincial Relations in Canadian Immigration." *Canadian Public Administration,* Vol. 30, No. 2 (Summer 1987): 299–317.

Vineberg, Robert, "Welcoming Immigrants at the Gateway to Canada's West: Immigration Halls in Winnipeg, 1872–1975." *Manitoba History,* No. 65 (Winter 2011): 13–22.

Webb, Sidney and Beatrice. *English Poor Law Policy (Volume 10 of English Local Government),* (1910). London: Frank Cass, 1963.

Whittaker, Reg. *Canadian Immigration Policy Since Confederation,* Booklet 15 in *Canadian Ethnic Groups.* Ottawa: Canadian Historical Association, 1991.

Wordsworth, James S. *Strangers Within Our Gates, or Coming Canadians,* 2nd Edition. Toronto: Methodist Mission Rooms, 1909.

Endnotes

Preface

1. Craig, Gerald E, editor, *Lord Durham's Report, An Abridgement of the Report on the Affairs of British North America* (Toronto and Montreal: McClelland and Stewart, 1963) 126.
2. LAC, Cabinet Conclusions, RG, PCO, Series A-5-a, Vol. 6436, June 6, 1974, 6.

Pre-Confederation Settlement Activities

1. Choquette, Leslie, "Recruitment of French Emigrants to Canada 1600–1760" in *To Make America – European Emigration in the Early Modern Period,* editors Ida Altman, and James Horn 131–171, (Berkeley and Los Angeles: University of California Press, 1991),138.
2. Nova Scotia, *1 Geo III, Cap. 6,* 1761 in *The statutes at large passed in the several general assemblies held in His Majesty's province of Nova-Scotia from the first assembly which met at Halifax the second day of October, in the thirty-second year of His late Majesty Geo. II. A.D. 1758, to the forty-fourth year of His present Majesty Geo. III. A.D. 1804, inclusive; with a complete index and abridgement of the whole* (Halifax: King's Printer, 1805), 21; and, Lower Canada, *An Act to oblige ships and vessels coming from places infected with the plague or any pestilential fever or disease, to perform* Quarantine, *and prevent the communication thereof in this Province, 35 Geo III, Cap. V,* 1795, in *Provincial Statutes of Lower Canada* (Québec: William Vondenvelden, 1795), 124–136.
3. Committee on the Survey of the Coasts, &c. of Scotland, *First Report: Emigration* (London: House of Commons, 1803), 4, 5.
4. United Kingdom, *43 Geo III, Cap.56,* cited in Kelley, Ninette and Trebilcock, Michael, *The Making of the Mosaic—A History of Canadian Immigration Policy* (Toronto: University of Toronto Press, 1998), 42.

5. Great Britain, *9 Geo IV, Cap. XXI, 1828.*

6. *Circular Dispatch* from Lord Goderich to Governors of Lower Canada, Nova Scotia and New Brunswick, December 11, 1831, in *North America:- Emigration. Return to an Address to His Majesty, dated 1 August 1832, for, Copy of any acts passed by the Colonies in British North America, and which have received His Majesty's Sanction, by which a Tax is to be levied on Emigrants arriving from the United Kingdom:- also, copy of circular from the Colonial Office, recommending the same.* House of Commons, London, 1832, Early Canadiana Online: http://canadiana.org/ECO/ItemRecord/9_01016?id=65526e55356767ce (accessed January 14, 2010).

7. Nova Scotia, *2 William IV, Cap. XVIII, An Act relating to Passengers from Great-Britain and Ireland, arriving in this Province,* 1832, in *Statutes of the Province of Nova Scotia, Vol. 4* (Halifax: King's Printer, 1835), 151–153; Lower Canada, *An Act to Create a Fund for defraying the expense of providing Medical assistance for sick Emigrants, and of enabling Indigent Persons of that description to proceed to the place of their destination, 2 William IV, Cap. XVII,* 1832 in *Provincial Statutes of Lower Canada* (Québec: J.C. Fisher & W. Kemble, 1832), 376–387; and, New Brunswick, *An Act, to regulate Vessels arriving from the United Kingdom with Passengers and Emigrants, 2 William IV, Cap. XXXVI,* 1832 in *The Acts of the General Assembly of Her Majesty's Province of Brunswick, from the Twenty Sixth Year of the Reign of King George the Third to the Sixth Year of the Reign of King William the Fourth* (Fredericton: Queen's Printer, 1838), 587, 588.

8. Upper Canada, *AN ACT granting a sum of money for the relief of sick and destitute Emigrants at Prescott, 2 William IV, Cap XXXIV,* 1832 in *The Statutes of Upper Canada, to the time of the Union, Vol. I —Public Acts* (Toronto: R. Stanton, 1843), 562.

9. Lower Canada, *An Act to establish Boards of Health within the Province, and to enforce an effectual system of Quarantine, 2 William IV, Cap. XVI,* February 25th, 1832, in *Provincial Statutes of Lower Canada* (Québec: J.C. Fisher & W. Kemble, 1832), 1832, pp 358–376; Nova Scotia, *An Act to prevent the spreading of Contagious Diseases, and for the performance of Quarantine, 2 William IV, Cap. XIII,* April 14th, 1832 in *Statutes of the Province of Nova Scotia, Vol. 4* (Halifax: King's Printer, 1835), 135–146; and, New Brunswick, *An Act to prevent the importation and spreading of infectious Distempers in the City of Saint John, 3 William IV, Cap XXI,* March 19th, 1833, in *The Acts of the General Assembly of Her Majesty's Province of Brunswick, from the Twenty Sixth Year of the Reign of King George the Third to the Sixth Year of the Reign of King William the Fourth* (Fredericton, Queen's Printer, 1838), 611–618.

10. Minister of Agriculture, *Report for the Calendar Year 1892* (Ottawa: Queen's Printer, 1893), xxx, xxxi.

11. Lower Canada, *An Act to appropriate a certain Sum of Money therein-mentioned, for the Relief of Indigent Sick Emigrants from the United Kingdom, 3 George IV, Cap. VII,* 1823, in *Provincial Statutes of Lower Canada* (Québec: P. E. Desbarats, 1823), 278–282.

12. Department of Citizenship and Immigration, *Developments in Canadian Immigration*, 154–176, in Dominion Bureau of Statistics, *Canada Year Book, 1957–58* (Ottawa Queen's Printer, 1958), 166.
13. *Lord Durham's Report*, 125.
14. *Lord Durham's Report*, 126.
15. Sidney and Beatrice Webb, *English Poor Law Policy, English Local Government, Vol. 10* (1910, London: Frank Cass, 1963), 19.
16. Province of Canada, *5 Victoria, Cap XIII, An Act to create a Fund for defraying the expense of enabling indigent Emigrants to proceed to their place of destination, and of supporting them until they can procure employment,* 1841, in *The Provincial Statutes of Canada* (Kingston: S. Derbishire and G. Desbarats, 1841), 71–75.
17. Province of Canada, *11 Victoria, Cap. I, An Act to make better provision with respect to Emigrants, and for defraying the expenses of supporting Indigent Emigrants, and of forwarding them to their place of destination, and to amend the Act therein mentioned,* 1848, in *Provincial Statutes of Canada* (Montreal: S. Derbishire and G. Desbarats, 1848), 5–10.
18. Province of Canada, *12 Victoria, Cap VI, An Act to repeal certain Acts therein mentioned, and to make further provision respecting Emigrants,* 1849, in *Provincial Statutes of Canada* (Montreal: S. Derbishire and G. Desbarats, 1849), 111–119.
19. Province of Canada, *16 Victoria, Cap. LXXXVI, An Act to amend and consolidate the Laws relative to Emigrants and Quarantine,* 1852, in *Statutes of the Province of Canada,* (Québec: S. Derbishire and G. Desbarats, 1852), 296–310.
20. Province of Canada, *22 Victoria, Cap. III, An Act to amend the law relating to Emigrants,* 1858, in *Statutes of the Province of Canada* (Québec: S. Derbishire and G. Desbarats, 1858), 7–10.
21. Province of Canada, *Consolidated Statutes of Canada, Cap. 40, An Act Respecting Emigrants and Quarantine* (Ottawa: Queen's Printer, 1866).

Post-Confederation Settlement Activities to 1945

1. *CYB* 1868, 80.
2. LAC, OiC, *PC1868-0981*, December, 18, 1868.
3. HoC, *Debates, Vol. II,* 1869, 460, 520, 521, 590, 929.
4. Canada, *Statutes of Canada, 32–33 Vict., Cap X,* 1869, *An Act respecting Immigration and Immigrants* (Ottawa: Queen's Printer, 1869), 32–46.
5. Canada, *Statutes of Canada, 35 Vict., Cap X,* 1872, *An Act to provide for the incorporation of Immigration Aid Societies* (Ottawa: Queen's Printer, 1872).
6. M&I, *Memorandum from Chief Programs Section to A/Director Programs and Procedures Branch re Immigrant Aid Societies Act,* August 26, 1968, LAC RG 76 Vol. 1306, File 5865-1 Settlement of Immigrants—General.

7. LAC, OiC, PC1872-0062B, June 21, 1872.
8. Robert Vineberg, 'Welcoming Immigrants at the Gateway to Canada's West: Immigration Halls in Winnipeg, 1872–1975', *Manitoba History*, No. 65 (Winter 2011), 14–22 passim.
9. New York Times, *Bruce Walker, Autocrat of Canada's Immigrants,* October 15, 1911.
10. LAC, OiC, *PC1872-0448*, May 11, 1872.
11. Minister of the Interior, *Annual Report for 1893 (calendar year)* (Ottawa: Queen's Printer, 1894), xi–xii.
12. LAC, OiCs, *PC1897-0771,* April 5, 1897; *PC1904-8078,* May 16, 1904; *PC1904-1419,* July 20, 1904; *PC1905-1565 and 1566,* August 10, 1905; and *PC1906-2111,* December 12, 1906.
13. Canada, *Acts of the Parliament of the Dominion of Canada, 6 Edward VII, Chap. 19, An Act respecting Immigration and Immigrants,* 1906 (Ottawa: Queen's Printer, 1906), 109–126.
14. LAC, OiCs, *PC1908-0028,* January 8, 1908, and *PC1908-0656,* March 27, 1908.
15. New York Times, *100,000 of our Farmers are Coaxed to Canada Every Year,* September 14, 1911.
16. Minister of Immigration and Colonization, *Annual Report 1924–25* (Ottawa: King's Printer, 1926), 7.
17. LAC, RG76 , Immigration ,Series I-A-1 , Volume 262 , Reel C-7810, File: 216882, *Joint agreement between Canadian Pacific Railway, Canadian National Railways and Department relating to immigration.*
18. Minister of Immigration and Colonization, *Annual Report 1928–29, 6, 7.*
19. Minister of Immigration and Colonization, *Annual Report 1924–25, 47–50.*
20. Minister of Immigration and Colonization, *Annual Reports 1924–25 to 1927–28.*
21. Minister of Immigration and Colonization, *Annual Report 1925–26, 25.*
22. Minister of Immigration and Colonization, *Annual Report 1926–27, 6.*

The Settlement Service

1. The new department also took on responsibility for 'Indian Affairs', as a goal of the government was to bring Canada's aboriginal peoples to full citizenship, including the right to vote, which they did not have at that time. In fact the Indian Affairs Branch was the largest branch of the department.
2. Dominion Bureau of Statistics, *CYB, 1952–3,* (Ottawa: King's Printer, 1953), 165.
3. DCI, *Memorandum from Chief of Operations to Head, Secretariat,* February 3, 1961, LAC RG 76 Vol. 747, File 510-7, Settlement Services Administration.
4. DCI, *Report for the Fiscal Year Ending March 31, 1952* (Ottawa: Queen's Printer, 1952), 11.

5. DCI, *Memorandum from Director of Canadian Citizenship to Director of Immigration*, April 29, 1954, LAC RG 76 Vol. 747, File 511-2-022, Liaison between Citizenship and Immigration Branches.

6. DCI, *Memorandum from Acting Chief, Development Division to File*, November 10, 1965, LAC RG 76 Vol. 747, File 511-2-022, Liaison between Citizenship and Immigration Branches.

7. Jewish Immigrant Aid Society website—http://www.jias.org/JIAS/jiasweb.htm, Manitoba Interfaith Immigration Council website—http://www.miic.ca/history.aspx; COSTI Immigrant Services website—http://www.costi.org/whoweare/history.php; and, Centre social d'aide aux immigrants website - http://www.centrecsai.org/index.php?pid=42 (all accessed December 8, 2009).

8. LAC, Cabinet Conclusions, RG, PCO, Series A-5-a, Vol. 2646, December 13, 1950.

9. DCI, *Annual Report, 1958–1959*, 27.

10. DCI, "Integration of Postwar Immigrants," *CYB 1959*, 176,7.

11. DCI, *Annual Report, 1958–1959*, 11; and, *Annual Report, 1959-1960*, 10.

12. DCI, *Annual Report, 1958–1959*, 24; and *Annual Report, 1959-1960*, 25.

13. DCI, *Immigration Policy Manual*, 1964, Section F, 1.

14. Ibid., Section F, 8.

15. LAC, Cabinet Conclusions, RG2, PCO, Series A-5-a, Vol. 2645, June 27, 1950, pp 2, 3.

16. *Fairclough to Starr*, October 30, 1958, reproduced in Department of Citizenship and Immigration, *Immigration Policy Manual*, 1964, Section F, 5 and 6.

17. HoC *Debates*, Vol. II, 1960-61, February 10, 1961, 1949, 50.

18. DCI, *Immigration Policy Manual*, 1964, Section F, 6.

19. DCI, *Annual Report, 1965–66*, 1.

20. HoC, *Debates*, Vol. 5, 1966, May 9, 1966, 4872.

21. Ibid., 4891.

22. CIC, *Immigrant Integration in Canada: Policy Objectives, Program Delivery and Challenges*, a draft for discussion prepared by Integration Branch, CIC, in 2001, 5.

23. Hawkins, Freda, *Canada and Immigration, Public Policy and Public Concern* (Montreal and London: McGill-Queen's University Press, 1972), 153.

24. M&I, *The Immigration Program*, Volume 2 of the Report of the Canadian Immigration and Population Study (Ottawa: Information Canada, 1974), 122.

25. Kent, Tom, *A Public Purpose, An Experience of Liberal Opposition and Canadian Government* (Kingston and Montreal: McGill-Queen's University Press, 1988), 398, 399.

26. Chief, Operations Branch to All District Superintendents, all Posts Abroad, *Use of the term "Settlement Service"*, June 2, 1954, LAC RG 76 Vol. 747, File 510-7 Settlement Services Administration.

27. DCI, *Personnel Information Circular No. 26*, March 1965, LAC RG 76 Vol 747, File 511-1, Departmental Administration.

Creation of the Settlement Program

1. M&I, Memorandum from Deputy Minister *Re: Proposed Task Force on Immigration Settlement,* March 21st, 1969, LAC RG 76 Vol. 747, File 511-2-022, Liaison Between Immigration & Citizenship Branches.
2. LAC, Cabinet Conclusions, RG2, PCO, Series A-5-a, Vol. 6436, June 6, 1974, 5, 6.
3. Ibid., 10.
4. M&I, *Memorandum to the Minister,* dated July 11, 1975, in LAC, RG76, Vol.736, Settlement Branch Documents (no file number).
5. M&I, Anticipated Oral Question, dated April 23, 1976, *Are funds for voluntary organizations being increased in 1976–77?* in LAC RG76, Vol. 1306, File 5865-1, Settlement of Immigrants-General.
6. M&I, *The Immigration Program,* Volume 2 of the Report of the Canadian Immigration and Population Study (Ottawa: Information Canada, 1974), 119–141 *passim.*
7. M&I/E&I, *Annual Reports,* 1976–77 to 1983–84. For 1974–75 and 1975–76, see note 4 above.
8. CIC, *Immigrant Integration in Canada: Policy Objectives, Program Delivery and Challenges,* a draft for discussion prepared by Integration Branch, CIC in 2001, 5.
9. LAC, Cabinet Conclusions, RG2, PCO, Series A-5-a, Vol. 6436, June 6, 1974, 5.
10. M&I, *The Immigration Program, Volume 2 of the Report of the Canadian Immigration and Population Study* (Ottawa: information Canada, 1974), 129
11. The author was hired as one of four summer students to provide a settlement service at the Ottawa Canada Manpower Centre in the summer of 1972. The new manager of CMC Ottawa had recently moved from Montreal where he had managed the settlement service at CMC Montreal Central and he was astonished that he had no such unit in Ottawa. With no budget to create a unit, he used his summer student budget instead and from May through August 1972, immigrants arriving in Ottawa were welcomed by summer students!

Constitutional Issues and Settlement in Quebec

1. Government of Quebec, *Draft Agreement on the Constitution—Proposals by the Government of Québec* (Quebec: Government of Quebec, 1985), 29, http://www.saic.gouv.qc.ca/publications/Positions/Part3/Document20_en.pdf (accessed October 2, 2008). The official French language version is: "La Constitution devra compléter l'entente Cullen-Couture de 1978 en confirmant la préponderance du Québec en matière de sélection et en élargissant cette préponderance à l'integration et a l'établissement des immigrants." Gouvernement du Québec, *Project d'accord Constitutionnel* (Québec: Gouvernement du Québec, 1985), 29.

http://www.saic.gouv.qc.ca/publications/Positions/Partie3/Document20.pdf (accessed October 2, 2008).

2. *The 1987 Constitutional Accord* (Meech lake Accord), Canadian Encyclopedia online, http://www.thecanadianencyclopedia.com/index.cfm?PgNm=TCE& Params=A1ARTA0010100 (accessed October 1, 2008).

3. Gall, Gerald L., *Meech Lake Accord*, Canadian Encyclopedia online, http://www.thecanadianencyclopedia.com/index.cfm?PgNm=TCE&Params= A1SEC824207 (accessed October 1, 2008).

4. *Consensus Report on the Constitution*, August 28, 1992, Final Text (Charlottetown Accord), Canadian Encyclopedia online, http://www.thecanadianencyclopedia. com/index.cfm?PgNm=TCE&Params=A1ARTA0010099 (accessed October 1, 2008).

5. McConnell, W.H. and Gall, Gerald L., *Constitutional History*, Canadian Encyclopedia—http://www.thecanadianencyclopedia.com/index.cfm?PgNm= TCE&Params=A1SEC818742 (accessed October 1, 2008).

6. Canada–Québec Accord relating to Immigration and Temporary Admission of Aliens (Canada-Quebec Accord) http://www.cic.gc.ca/english/department/laws-policy/agreements/quebec/can-que.asp (accessed October 1, 2008).

7. Penny Becklumb, *Immigration: The Canada-Quebec Accord, BP-252E,* Law and Government Division, Parliamentary Research Branch (Ottawa: Library of Parliament, 2008), 3, http://www.parl.gc.ca/information/library/PRBpubs/ bp252-e.pdf (accessed March 13, 2011).

8. Ibid., 5.

9. CIC, *Government of Canada 2011–12 settlement funding allocations,* http://www. cic.gc.ca/english/department/media/backgrounders/2010/2010-12-07.asp (accessed March 13, 2011).

Repatriation of the Settlement Program

1. E&I, *Annual Report to Parliament, Immigration Plan for 1991–1995, Year Two,* (Ottawa: 1991), 6.

2. Ibid., 7.

3. CIC, *Immigrant Integration in Canada: Policy Objectives, Program Delivery and Challenges*, a draft for discussion prepared by Integration Branch, CIC in 2001, 5, 6.

4. Interview with James Crawford, January 10, 2010.

5. Interview with Ian Glen, January, 6, 2010.

Settlement Renewal

1. SCCI, November 28, 1995, http://www.parl.gc.ca/35/Archives/committees351/ cits/evidence/103_95-11-28/cits103_blk101.html (accessed December 8, 2009).

2. Ibid.

3. CIC, *Departmental Outlook on Program Expenditures and Priorities, 1995-96 to 1997-98,* (Ottawa: 1995), 8.

4. Canadian Council for Refugees, Canadian National Settlement Service Standards Framework, 2000, http://www.ccrweb.ca/standards.htm#HISTORICAL CONTEXT (accessed December 8, 2009).

5. Department of Finance, *Getting Government Right - Program Review Overview,* Budget 1995 Fact Sheet 6, http://www.fin.gc.ca/budget95/fact/FACT_6e.html (accessed October 2, 2008).

6. CIC, *Performance Report for the period ending March 31, 1997* (Ottawa: Supply and Services Canada, 1997), 18, and *Report on Plans and Priorities, 1998–99* (Ottawa: Supply and Services Canada, 1998), 28.

7. CIC, *Performance Report for the period ending March 31, 1999* (Ottawa: Supply and Services Canada, 1999), 26.

8. Auditor General of Canada, *December 2001 Report to Parliament,* Chapter 5, Voted Grants and Contributions—Program Management, paragraph 5.136, http://www.oag-bvg.gc.ca/internet/English/parl_oag_200112_05_e_11826.html#ch5hd3g (accessed December 10, 2009).

9. BC Coalition for Immigrant Integration, *Inter-Provincial Report Card on Immigrant Settlement & Labour Market Integration Services,* Executive Summary, May 2002, http://74.125.95.132/search?q=cache:lIvkuIM5gwgJ:www.ocasi.org/downloads/Report%2520Card%2520-%2520Exec%2520Summary%2520(8.5X11).doc+Immigrant+Settlement+Funding+British+Columbia&cd=1&hl=en&ct=clnk&gl=ca (accessed December 8, 2009).

Solving the Funding Issues

1. Ontario, Legislative Assembly, *Official Records for 9 May 2005,* 1400 h http://www.ontla.on.ca/web/house-proceedings/house_detail.do?Date=2005-05-09&Parl=38&Sess=1&locale=en#P227_23789 (accessed March 13, 2011).

2. Canada-Ontario Immigration Agreement, http://www.cic.gc.ca/english/department/laws-policy/agreements/ontario/ont-2005-agree.asp (accessed October 7, 2008).

3. Ibid., Section 8.

4. CTV.ca, *Albertans claim victory after Conservative win,* January 24, 2006, http://www.ctv.ca/servlet/ArticleNews/story/CTVNews/20060124/west_reaction_060124/20060124?hub=Canada (accessed October 8, 2008).

5. Affiliation of Multicultural Societies and Services Agencies of BC, *Federal Immigrant Funding Increases,* in the AMSSA Insider, December 2005, http://www.amssa.org/updates/amssainsiderdecember2005.pdf (accessed October 8, 2008).

6. CIC, *Settlement Funding Allocations,* http://www.cic.gc.ca/English/department/media/backgrounders/2006/2006-11-10.asp (accessed October 8, 2008).

7. CIC, *Settlement Funding Allocations for 2008-09,* http://www.cic.gc.ca/english/department/media/backgrounders/2007/2007-12-17.asp (accessed October 8, 2008).
8. CIC, *Government of Canada 2011–12 settlement funding allocations*, http://www.cic.gc.ca/english/department/media/backgrounders/2010/2010-12-07.asp (accessed March 13, 2011).
9. CIC, *Resettlement* web page, http://www.cic.gc.ca/English/refugees/reform-resettle.asp#tphpidtphp (accessed April 11, 2011).

Foreign Credential Recognition

1. Minister of Manpower and Immigration, *Canadian Immigration Policy: White Paper on Immigration* (Ottawa: Information Canada,1966), page 6, para. 16.
2. Internal Trade Secretariat, *Agreement on Internal Trade 1995,* Article 701, (Winnipeg: Internal Trade Secretariat, 2010), 83.
3. Internal Trade Secretariat, *AIT Annual Report 1999–2000,* Chapter 7, Labour Mobility, 3. AIT annual reports are available at http://www.ait-aci.ca/index_en/reports.htm (accessed December 10, 2009).
4. AIT, *Report 2002–2004,* Chapter 7, Labour Mobility, 6.
5. AIT, *Annual Report 2004–2005,* Chapter 7, Labour Mobility, 1, 2.
6. Government of Canada News Release, November 30, 2009, *Federal, provincial and territorial governments speed up foreign credential recognition for newcomers to Canada,* http://news.gc.ca/web/article-eng.do?m=%2Findex&nid=499119 (accessed December 10, 2009).
7. Human Resources and Skills Development Canada, *Pan-Canadian Framework for the Assessment and Recognition of Foreign Qualifications*, http://www.hrsdc.gc.ca/eng/workplaceskills/publications/fcr/pcf.shtml (accessed December 10, 2009).
8. CIC, Foreign Credentials Referral Office, *Progress Report 2007-08,* http://www.credentials.gc.ca/about/progress-report2007.asp (accessed December 10, 2009).
9. CIC, Foreign Credentials Referral Office, *Progress Report 2009,* http://www.credentials.gc.ca/about/progress-report2009.asp (accessed March 13, 2011).

Emerging Issues and the New Terms and Conditions

1. Government of Canada, *The Next Act: New Momentum For Canada's Linguistic Duality —The Action Plan For Official Languages* (Ottawa: Government of Canada, 2003), 45.
2. Comité directeur Citoyenneté et Immigration Canada—Communautés francophones en situation minoritaire, *Plan stratégique pour favoriser l'immigration au sein des communautés francophones en situation minoritaire* (Ottawa: 2006), 6.

3. CIC, *Report on the Evaluation of the Delivery of the Canadian Orientation Abroad Initiative*, http://www.cic.gc.ca/EnGLish/resources/evaluation/orientation. asp (accessed December 10, 2009).

4. International Organization for Migration, *Canadian Orientation Abroad: Helping Future Immigrants Adapt to Life in Canada*, http://www.iom.int/jahia/ Jahia/canadian-orientation-abroad (accessed March 13, 2010).

5. Centre for Community Based Research, *Canadian Immigrant Integration Program (CIIP) Pilot —Final Evaluation Report* (Kitchener: Centre for Community Based Research, 2010), 11.

6. Canadian Immigrant Integration Project, *Final Report on Statistics for the CIIP Pilot*, 1, http://www.newcomersuccess.ca/images/stories/StatsRPTJul07-Sept10.pdf (accessed March 13, 2011).

7. Centre for Community Based Research, *Canadian Immigrant Integration Program (CIIP) Pilot—Final Evaluation Report,* 33-41.

8. Canadian Immigrant Integration Project, *What is CIIP?* http://www. newcomersuccess.ca/index.php/en/about-ciip (accessed March 13, 2011).

9. CIC and Ontario Minister of Citizenship and Immigration, *Call for Proposals – Local Immigration Partnerships,* At Work Settlement.org, http://atwork. settlement.org/downloads/atwork/CIC_MCI_CFP_LIP.pdf (accessed April 9, 2011).

10. CIC, Integration Branch, *Settlement Program, Implementation of the Modernized Approach*, PowerPoint presentation, 2009, 15.

11. PCO, OiC - *PC 2008-1732*, October 30, 2008, http://www.pco-bcp.gc.ca/oic-ddc.asp?lang=eng&Page=secretariats&txtOICID=&txtFromDate=2008-10-01& txtToDate=2008-10-31&txtPrecis=Multiculturalism&txtDepartment=&txtAct= &txtChapterNo=&txtChapterYear=&txtBillNo=&rdoComingIntoForce=&Do Search=Search+%2F+List (accessed December 14, 2009).

12. CIC, *Departmental Performance Report*, period ending March 31, 2009 (Ottawa: Public Works and Government Services, 2009), 16, 32.

Index

R. Vineberg, *Responding to Immigrants' Settlement Needs: The Canadian Experience*,   89
SpringerBriefs in Population Studies, DOI: 10.1007/978-94-007-2688-8,
© The Author(s) 2012